*The Art of Salad Making*

*Other Cookbooks by Carol Truax*


THE 60 MINUTE CHEF (*with Lillian Bueno McCue*)

LADIES' HOME JOURNAL COOKBOOK (*Editor*)

THE WEEKEND CHEF

LADIES' HOME JOURNAL DESSERT COOKBOOK (*Editor*)

FATHER WAS A GOURMET

THE CATTLEMAN'S STEAKBOOK (*with S. Oscar Barker*)

# THE ART OF
# *Salad Making*

## BY CAROL TRUAX

Illustrated by
JEAN CHARLOT

DOUBLEDAY & COMPANY, INC.

GARDEN CITY, NEW YORK

# Contents

I   SALAD ON THE MENU                                            11

    *Menus*                                                      17

    Luncheon                                                     17

    Dinner                                                       20


II  AMERICA IS THE SALAD BOWL OF THE WORLD                       23

    *Lettuces and Salad Greens*                                  25

       RECIPES

    Green and Mixed Tossed Salads                                29

    Platter Salads                                               34

    Chef's Salads                                                36

    Vegetable Salads                                             42

    Raw Vegetable Salads                                         50

    Poultry and Meat Salads                                      62

    Fish Salads                                                  68

    Molded Salads                                                81

    Fruit Salads                                                 90

    Dessert Salads                                               98


III SALAD DAYS AROUND THE GLOBE                                 105

       RECIPES

    French Salads                                               108

    Italian Salads                                              111

    Swiss Salads                                                116

    German Salads                                               118

    Scandinavian Salads                                         122

    Spanish and Mexican Salads                                  127

South American Salads                          132
Russian Salads                                 136
Near Eastern Salads                            139
Oriental Salads                                145

IV   WHAT THE WELL-DRESSED SALAD WILL WEAR      153
*Herbs for Salads*                             158
*Spices and Seeds for Salads*                  160
     RECIPES
French Dressing and Variations                 163
Mayonnaise and Variations                      170
Cooked Dressings                               178
Roquefort Dressings                            181
Dairy Dressings                                183
Bonus Dressings                                187

INDEX                                          195

*The Art of Salad Making*

\* To locate recipes designated with an asterisk and/or initial Capital Letters consult the Index.

# Chapter One

## SALAD ON THE MENU

My father was by profession a judge of the State Supreme Court, and by avocation a judge of good food. When he came home from the courthouse, he would doff his high silk hat, and his otter-collared greatcoat, and come to the nursery to continue my education in the things that mattered.

The way any other parent might take a child on his knee and nourish the growing mind by reading aloud from improving works, my father would take me on his broad lap and nourish me with choice tidbits, a succulent snail, an oyster Rockefeller, or an artichoke heart, improving my mind the while with a grave and expert discourse on gustatory lore. Escoffier was always more real to me than Brer Rabbit. In such sessions he taught me to appreciate the place of salad on the menu long before my time. At an age when other American moppets were protesting, in the classic phrase, "I say it's spinach . . ." I was reaching eagerly for my broccoli vinaigrette. I was already turning up my nose at a meal without salad in the saladless age of Yankee gustatory innocence, many years ago.

I have been spreading the gospel of salad ever since. Like the apostles of old, I have had my moments of peril, and my almost-martyrdoms, while as a food lecturer I spread the good word.

There was the fatal day when I journeyed to Philadelphia to preach the art of the salad. A group had summoned me to take part in their series in which cookbook authors demonstrated their techniques. With a stack of copies of my *Weekend Chef* under my arm, I journeyed into the wilderness. The blizzard howled, the temperature dropped with a thud, as I struggled through the storm to the auditorium and began operations.

I was delighted to find that the last word in equipment had already been installed for my demonstration. I was equally delighted to find two very pretty young ladies ready to carry out my behests. They stood at attention like magician's assistants, one at the sink, one at the stove, as the crowded audience threw back their furs and rustled into silence, and the lecture started.

"Ladies," I said, "I will demonstrate the important art—and it is an art—of washing and drying salad greens. First we half-fill the sink with cold water—"

Assistant No. 1 turned on the spigot.

Nothing happened.

What can be wrong?

The pipes have burst!

Five minutes later, like Rebecca at the well, we were washing the greens in a pail of water.

"Thus we see," I advised solemnly, "that even if you live on the Main Line, it is good to have running water laid on in your kitchens."

"Now for a cooked dressing. Please turn on the gas under the double boiler."

Assistant No. 2 turned the control.

Nothing happened.

What can be wrong?

The gas line is frozen!

Five minutes later, I was compounding a sour cream dressing for the cole slaw. It was delicious.

"French dressing," I announced. "In these days of educated machines, nothing is easier than to buzz a dressing in a blender."

Assistant No. 1 manned the blender.

"Salt and pepper," I ordered. She put it in.

"Sugar—paprika—tarragon—"

She pinched and sprinkled.

"Vinegar—oil—"

"Cover the blender, and buzz."

My acolyte buzzed gently. The audience could see the appetizing mixture creaming against the glass.

"And now I'll taste it."

The assistant switched off the blender, uncapped it, and handed me a spoon.

"Mm—more tarragon? Yes, I think so, a dash."

She added a dash of tarragon.

"And now—blend once more—and *voilà!*" I said grandly, with a cordon bleu flourish.

The zealous assistant switched on the blender full speed—and the dressing, as the saying goes, hit the fan.

Out flew a fountain, ceiling high, and settled down again on everything, on my carefully coiffed head, on the young assistant's bubble hairdo, on shoulders and table and blender and salad bowl. Never had a food lecturer and her food been so marinated.

Not counting on such blind obedience, I had omitted to instruct my sorcerer's apprentice to re-cover the blender.

"Ladies," I added hastily, mopping dressing from my hair, my shoulders, and my shoes, "one more word about blending a dressing—always cover the blender!"

That tore it. The audience howled.

"And remember," I concluded, wiping off my eyelashes, "that salad is nature's gift to menu making!"

I have never given another demonstration to prove so graphically that you have to cover the blender; but every time I demonstrate the art of salad making, I prove that salads are the most versatile of foods. On your table they can do anything.

Take the standard menu of soup, meat-and-vegetable, and dessert. You can't have the dessert first or the soup last (unless you're Chinese), but salad can substitute for any of these courses in any position. It can also augment any course. In America, many a salad makes the whole meal.

In the restaurants of European countries, the salads are often listed with the first course, the *antipasto,* the Vorspeise, the *hors d'oeuvres.* There salad does on a plate what the aperitif does in a glass: it whets, not satiates, the appetite.

That is why the menu-maker chooses a light salad to begin the meal: an aspic, seafood, fruit, something green, anything slight and piquant. This salad is only the overture. The opus is to follow.

Perhaps, instead, you choose to serve your salad with or immediately following the main course, as a grace note to the opus. For a grace note, there is nothing like a green or tossed salad.

Such a salad can be served right on the dinner plate, where it exchanges its good flavors with the juice from the roast beef, or the wine sauce from the chicken casserole.

A stuffed tomato or artichoke or other sculpture, topped with mayonnaise or vinaigrette, goes better on a salad plate by itself, and may be served following the main course rather than along with it.

The green salad, with or without cheese and crackers, is equally delightful as a course by itself following the main dish.

Any salad served in mid-meal, in association with the main course, must be considered as part of that course, and carefully chosen to go with it, considering texture and taste as well as color. I'll have more to say about this point as we go along.

Then there is the dessert salad, which crowns the meal with something light and refreshing, whether it is sweet or not. For this purpose, mousses and aspics are ideal; but the greatest of all is blended fruits. Here is your chance to balance your whole meal, to tie it up and pull it together in a memorable finale. As you rise from the table, the beautiful dessert is the latest impression of your eye and the taste you carry in your mouth.

Sometimes a salad can be so good, and so substantial, that you want to give it your entire attention. Many salads take the whole spotlight for luncheon or supper, or as the main meal on a very hot day. An ideal choice is a bountiful chef's salad, an American term loosely used for a salad of greens and vegetables with a generous scattering of smoked or other meat, chicken, fish or shellfish, and slivered cheese. Equally suited to absorb the whole attention would be a shrimp, crab, or lobster salad, a roast beef salad, or a chicken salad, still the queen of them all.

There is also the huge platter salad, which looks so good, and suits itself so well to every taste, as each one helps himself to exactly the right amount of exactly the things he likes best, such as: sliced or slivered meat, flaked or salted fish, cooked or raw vegetables, and assorted greens.

As you put together your handsome platter salad, and present it to the admiring eyes and the appreciative palates of your family and guests, you realize anew that the salad maker is an artist. Every salad you serve is a picture you have painted, a sculpture you have modeled, a drama you have created.

Warning to food artists: Don't get carried away! Don't be over dramatic or over colorful, the platter must look appetizing and the salad taste good.

The hostess who gets carried away is a dreadful menace, and most of all to the cookbook writer. The food expert can't win. Half the world won't invite you to eat because you scare them. The other half has to show off.

"You write cookbooks, so you must taste my marshmallow surprise with pink dressing—my tomato and raisin treat—my banana special—"

No escape. She served the banana special. When I saw it I thought it was an oversized caterpillar; but it turned out to be a whole banana drenched in honey and rolled—believe it or not—in cornflakes.

"You *must* have the recipe." She had it ready for me. I'm afraid I lost it.

Food, then, is made to eat, not to look at. But appearance contributes to taste, and precedes it. Every good thing you put into your mouth, you have looked at first, and at sight of the artistry of its presentation and the harmony of its color and form, you have already begun to enjoy it. This is especially true of your salad course.

The beauty of a well-constructed salad is more than skin deep: it is a promise of the taste sensation to come. The eye reacts to color before the palate experiences flavor; and rightly so, because color goes hand in hand with taste.

When you vary the flavor of a dish, you are likely to find you have changed the color as well. The natural rich yellow of that mayonnaise looks appetizing on the red and white of cold lobster; and it tastes right too. Herb mayonnaise goes better with cold salmon; and it takes on a fresh green color which strikes a high note against the frosty pink of the chilled fish. Tomatoed mayonnaise dressing is subtle enough to enhance without overpowering the delicate flavor of crab meat. It pleases the eye equally with the accent of pink dressing against white meat edged with red.

With a platter of cold seafood, the salad artist may offer three shades of dressing at once, in a triple dish, or in three little saucers. The three bright colors, yellow, green, and frosty pink, make a pleasing combination to lift the spirits and whet the appetite.

It is important to remember the principle of contrast in choosing and decorating your salad vegetables. They should contrast with one another, and with the rest of the menu, both to refresh the eye, and because the color contrast ensures flavor variety also.

There's no use making your guests see red by surrounding a Westphalian ham with consommé Madrilene, buttered beets, tomato aspic, and watermelon. Nor need you give them creeping anemia with a repast of cream of celery soup, breast of chicken, mashed potatoes, hearts of palm salad, and vanilla ice cream. With your chicken you could just as well serve the bright tomato aspic, and keep the subtle pastel hearts of palm to adorn the ham.

In short, when you are fitting a salad into the menu, you are decorating the exterior as well as the interior. You are painting a picture with your palette of eatables as well as tickling the palates of the eaters. You are calling upon your artistry of eye and nose and taste buds to appeal to the same senses in others.

The following favorite menus of mine are for guidance only, suggesting what can be done by the salad course to add sparkle and life to the meal, to provide the taste touch, to add the refining and decorating supplement to the bill of fare. They prove that a meal becomes a dinner, a lunch becomes a luncheon, when the right salad is included. Salads do honor to the guests. Mix and match your own as your inventiveness indicates.

# Menus

Use the following menus as guides,
it's fun to plan your own.

## LUNCHEON MENUS

Baked Macaroni and Cheese
Green Salad, Chicken Liver Dressing
Frozen Fruit Salad

❦

Broiled Fish
Stuffed Tomatoes
Ice Cream Cake

❦

Chicken Broth
Tomato Aspic with Seafood
English Muffins
Pears and Cheese

❦

Baked Grapefruit
Caesar Salad
French Rolls
Spanish Cream

❦

Cold Roast Beef
Hearts of Palm Salad
Melba Toast
Hot Baked Pears

ॐ

Clam Broth
Chef's Salad
French Bread
Crème Caramel

ॐ

Platter Salad
Hot Rolls
Apple Pie

ॐ

Consommé
Gazpacho Salad
Hot Biscuits
Chocolate Roll

ॐ

Shrimp, Crab, or Lobster Salad
Toasted Crackers
Raspberry Sherbet
Pound Cake

ॐ

Mushroom Soup
Fruit Salad
Crackers
Irish Coffee Ice Cream

ಳಿ

Fruit Cup
Broiled Sweetbreads
Tossed Green Salad
Chocolate Roll

ಳಿ

Tomato Juice
Eggs Benedict
Spinach Salad
Strawberry Shortcake

ಳಿ

Oyster Soup
Artichokes Vinaigrette
Strawberry Tart

## DINNER MENUS

Oyster Cocktail
Roast Turkey
Glazed Onions    Mashed Potatoes
Cole Slaw with Grapes
Pumpkin Pie

ಞ

Lobster Cocktail
Roast Pheasant
Fois Gras Toast    Pilaf    Braised Endive
Grapefruit and Orange Salad
Vanilla Soufflé

ಞ

Smoked Salmon with Capers
Pot Roast
Potato Pancakes, Applesauce
Cooked Vegetable Salad
Lemon Sherbet

ಞ

Turtle Soup
Roast Beef
Cauliflower    Roast Potatoes
Tomato Salad
Crème Brûlée

ಞ

Melon Prosciutto
Baked Fish
New Potatoes    Green Beans with Almonds
Cucumber Salad
Chocolate Mousse

ೞ

Pea Soup
Fried Chicken
Spoon Bread    Asparagus
Water Cress Salad
Chocolate Cake

ೞ

Fruit Salad
Baked Ham
Asparagus in Mustard Sauce    Sweet Potatoes
Cole Slaw
Cheese Cake

ೞ

Tomato Aspic with Vegetables
Chicken Fricassee
Dumplings    Green Beans
Hot Fruit Compote    Cookies

ೞ

Crab Meat Cocktail
Broiled Steak
French Fried Potatoes    Mushrooms
Avocado Salad
Strawberry Pie

ೞ

Melon

Roast Pork

Brussels Sprouts        Baked Onions

Waldorf Salad

Coffee Ice Cream

&

Seafood Salad

Roast Leg of Lamb

Puree of Peas        Roasted Potatoes

Green Salad, Anchovy Dressing

Meringue Ring with Fruit

# Chapter Two

## AMERICA IS THE SALAD BOWL
## OF THE WORLD

On many occasions those two great American institutions meet—
the salad luncheon and the literary lion.

I remember once when I was the lion, with a corsage on my
shoulder, *The Ladies' Home Journal Cookbook* at my elbow, and
chicken salad on my plate. I was glad to oblige the large group of
good ladies by eating their chicken salad and telling them about
my book.

When the affair ended, the chairman surprised me by produc-
ing a check. Out of the corner of my eye I could see that the
amount was negligible. I waved it away with a grand gesture.

"Oh, I'm here to promote my book, I couldn't take money!"

"No? Thank you very much. May we put it in our special fund?"

"Of course. What is your special fund for?"

"For getting better speakers next year."

This put me off lecturing free at American literary luncheons;
but nothing has ever put me off the American salad.

Salad is rapidly becoming the American national dish. American
salads are second to none, from the substantial meal salad to the
light tossed green salad. More and more calorie-conscious, the
American housewife increasingly favors salad, the dieter's chosen
food.

Americans abroad get homesick for their salads. Marketing for
salad greens in foreign lands is likely to be a disappointment except at exactly the right time and place. You get the fresh ingredients only at the peak of the salad-growing season, and the

best of these are found only in the regions where they grow. In many countries it is not advisable for Americans to eat raw vegetables. At home, shopping for salad is an adventure all year round. American expatriates begin to dream of their own supermarkets, colorfully stacked with salad ingredients of every description. We are indeed fortunate that nature—and the hybridizers—have been so generous in the many types of greens that are available to the salad maker.

Imagine one country offering such a variety of good things in salads: Florida citrus, Maine lobster, Colorado celery, Pacific Coast crab, Pennsylvania Dutch wilted greens, Hawaiian fruit-filled pineapple, California avocados on the half shell, Kentucky Bibb lettuce tossed in an herbed dressing.

The American green salad goes with everything. It is delicious made of soft Boston head lettuce, or bronze or other leaf lettuce. A contrast in texture and color adds interest, as when a crisp lettuce like iceberg, and dark green water cress or spinach are mixed. Endive or escarole adds a bitter tang as well as a changed texture.

# Lettuces and Salad Greens

Greens are called by various names in different places, some alternate names are given in parentheses.

BIBB (Limestone)  Miniature fragile heads, each leaf yellow to green, grows only in limestone soil—delicious, and not easily available, about the best lettuce in the world.

BOSTON (Butter, Simpson)  Sometimes erroneously called Bibb. A round loosely packed head, tender leaves, delicious and mild.

BRONZE (Red)  A garden lettuce similar in texture and taste to leaf lettuce, leaves edged with bronze.

CABBAGE  A firmly packed head of thick, heavy, pale green or purple-red leaves.

CHICORY (Curly Endive)  Feathery leaves that spread out, yellow at center, pale to darker green outside, crisp with a slightly bitter taste, mixes well with other greens.

DANDELION  Thin, long, arrowlike, dark green leaves, tart flavor.

ENDIVE (Belgian Endive)  Is a long, narrow, very pale yellow, firm head made of tightly packed, long, pointed, waxy leaves. Unusual tangy flavor.

ESCAROLE  Flat spread-out heads, yellow center to dark green edges, leaves are curly, firm, and rough-textured with a distinctive bitter taste.

FIELD LETTUCE (Lamb's Tongue)  Very small spears on delicate stems. Soft, delightful, not always available. Always worth buying.

ICEBERG (Head)  A round firm head lettuce, keeps well—is crisp, watery, and not flavorful.

LEAF LETTUCE (Garden Lettuce)  Soft long leaves with crumpled edges, tends to form heads, tender, fragile, and good. Does not keep or ship well. There are a number of varieties of leaf lettuce.

OAK LEAF (Salad Bowl, Australian) Soft oak-leaf shape, suede-like, pale to medium green leaves. A slightly tangy flavor.

ROMAINE A long narrow head, oval leaves dark green outside, yellow at the heart—firm, crisp, and juicy, a tasty lettuce that keeps well.

SPINACH Dark green leaves, some crinkly, on stems; use young spinach leaves only. A special flavor and good color contrast with other greens.

WATER CRESS Small stalks with numerous small, round, dark green petals; sold tied in bunches, strong lively taste, not bitter, an excellent addition to the salad bowl.

Salad greens must be washed. Firm lettuces may best be cleaned by cutting out the stem. Cut it out about an inch deep, not just off. Let cold water run briskly into this hole. To drip dry, turn the head right side up on the drainboard. Remove outside wilted leaves, pull the head apart, pat dry with a towel, and put in the refrigerator to crisp. Romaine lettuce, escarole, and other clusters of firm leaves may be pulled apart first, then washed, patted dry, and crisped in the refrigerator. Boston, field, and other soft lettuces are too delicate to be patted dry. After floating them in water, spread them out on a dish towel, brown paper, or paper toweling to dry in the air.

A French salad basket, in spite of its looks, isn't a birdcage. It's a wire gadget that gives a sporting touch to cleaning greens. Fill it, hang it on the faucet, and let the water stream through. Then, as you whirl the contraption wildly around your head you work off your aggressions and sprinkle the kitchen as you dry the lettuce. Your daily dozen done, let the greens stand in the basket until toss-time comes.

Wet lettuce tends to dilute the salad dressing. Sometimes you may choose to have your dressing thinned, in which case don't worry about drying the greens completely. On most occasions, lettuce shouldn't be wet. You don't want your potato salad to go swimming in the lettuce cup, and you never want your mayonnaise diluted.

If you are making a tossed salad, now is the time to prepare the greens into bite-size pieces. Take the washed lettuce, and tear it; be sure to tear, not cut. Only torn lettuce coats itself completely when turned in the dressing. Dry the pieces in a towel, and put towel and contents in the refrigerator to crisp. If your towel overflows, use a pillow case. It is so easy to dump the crisped green bites out of the moist cloth directly into your salad bowl. No fuss, no muss! It will keep fresh and crisp all day, so prepare it ahead of time.

In food photography the salad bowl is always heaped high to make a pretty picture. I defy anybody to toss that salad, or even to serve it, without sprinkling herbage all over the scenery. That doesn't mean that you can't make a pretty picture of your salad. You can and must. For any salad whose ingredients you wish to show off choose a low broad salad bowl or a deep platter. For a green salad to be tossed, use a deep bowl.

A wooden bowl for salad is the tradition, and if you really keep it clean, there is nothing against wood; but from time to time it must be scrubbed and set in the sun, to purge it of the stale garlic and rancid oil that lurk in the grain. For daily care, a swipe with a paper towel will do. Glass, plastic, or ceramic bowls are easy to take care of and lovely to look at. For a handsome salad, the prettier the container the better. Select one of generous size to toss your salad in, or you will find you have tossed it right onto the kitchen floor or the dining room table.

Finally, consider garlic. Wherever crushed garlic is called for, use a garlic press. In making salad dressing, you may crush the garlic with a fork, but remove it before serving.

# Green and Mixed Tossed Salads

### TOSSED GREEN SALAD
*(4 servings)*

1 quart torn assorted salad greens
2 teaspoons minced parsley
⅓ cup French Dressing*
2–3 tablespoons grated Parmesan cheese (optional)

Put the greens in a bowl. Mix the parsley into the French Dressing. Pour over the greens and toss. Top with cheese if you wish.


### MIXED GREEN SALAD
*(8 servings)*

1 head romaine
1 head chicory or escarole
4–5 heads Belgian endive
2 tablespoons minced chives or scallions
¼ cup minced parsley
½–¾ cup French Dressing*
¼ cup grated Cheddar cheese or Parmesan cheese (optional)

Wash and dry the greens thoroughly. Break the romaine and chicory or escarole into bite-size pieces and cut the endive. Put the greens in a bowl and sprinkle with chives and parsley. When ready to serve, pour the dressing over and toss thoroughly. Don't use too much dressing, just enough to coat the lettuce. Sprinkle with cheese if you wish.

### MIXED GREEN SALAD WITH RADISHES
*(6 servings)*

1 head lettuce
1 bunch radishes
4 tomatoes
2 hard boiled eggs
2 tablespoons chopped chives
¼ cup French Dressing*

Wash and dry the lettuce and break into bite-size pieces. Slice the radishes thin. Peel and slice the tomatoes and chop the eggs, keeping yolks and whites separate. Put the lettuce in a salad bowl and add the radishes and tomatoes. Top with the chopped or grated egg, put yolk in the center and white around the edge. Sprinkle with chives. Pour the dressing over and toss at the table.

### GREENS WITH ONIONS
*(6 servings)*

1 pound spinach
1 head lettuce
1 (3½ ounce) can French fried onions
½ cup French Dressing*

Wash the spinach thoroughly and pick it over. Dry thoroughly and break into bite-size pieces. Break the lettuce also, and toss together. Heat the onions and put over the top, and pour the dressing over all.

### ENDIVE SALAD
*(4 servings)*

1 pound Belgian endive
Few leaves soft lettuce (optional)
¼ cup French Dressing*
1 hard boiled egg, chopped or grated (garnish)

Wash the endive, remove any wilted leaves. Cut each head into quarters lengthwise and place on the greens. Serve with the dressing poured over and garnish if you wish with the egg.


## BELGIAN ENDIVE SALAD
(*4 servings*)

1  pound Belgian endive
10  anchovies
½  cup chopped water cress
¼  cup French Dressing*

Wash the endive, trim the root ends. Pull off a few outside leaves and put into a salad bowl. Cut centers in quarters lengthwise. Add to the bowl. Cut up 6 of the anchovies and mix with water cress and French Dressing. Pour over the salad and garnish with remaining anchovies rolled.


## ROMAINE SALAD BOWL
(*6 servings*)

2  heads romaine
2  bunches leaf lettuce
2  large tomatoes, peeled, cut in wedges
1  cucumber, sliced
1  avocado, peeled, sliced
6  scallions, chopped
⅓  cup French Dressing*
½  teaspoon dry tarragon or chervil

Tear the romaine and lettuce into bite-size pieces into a salad bowl. Add the tomatoes, cucumber, avocado, and scallions, and toss with French Dressing, and tarragon or chervil.

## FIELD SALAD
### (4 servings)

½  pound field lettuce
1  can tiny whole beets (optional)
¼  cup French Dressing*

Wash and dry the salad gently. Field salad is not too easy to come by and is delicious alone or in a mixed salad. Add the beets if you wish and toss with the French Dressing.

## MUSHROOM TOSSED GREENS
### (6 servings)

1  head romaine
1  head leaf lettuce
½  pound Belgian endive (optional)
½  pound mushrooms
½  cup Lemon French Dressing*

Wash and dry all the greens. Break them up and put in a bowl. Wipe the mushrooms and trim the end of the stems—if they are discolored, peel them. Slice them thin, stem and all. Put on top of the greens. Pour the dressing over and toss.

## SPINACH SALAD
### (4 servings)

1  pound spinach
1  teaspoon salt
1  tablespoon sugar
½  teaspoon paprika
½  teaspoon dry mustard
1  teaspoon Worcestershire sauce
2  tablespoons lemon juice
¼  cup catsup
1  cup oil
2  tablespoons vinegar

Wash the spinach in several waters, and remove hard stems. Cut
the spinach into strips, dry, and chill. Make the dressing by mixing
the salt, sugar, paprika, and mustard with Worcestershire sauce,
lemon juice, and catsup. Slowly add the oil and vinegar alternately
while beating in an electric mixer or with a rotary hand mixer.
The dressing should be thick. Stir in a lump of ice to ensure the
thickness. Serve over the spinach.

## SPINACH AND BACON SALAD
### (6 servings)

2 pounds spinach
3 hard boiled eggs, chopped
8 slices crisp cooked bacon, crumbled
⅓ cup Yogurt Dressing* or French Dressing*

Wash spinach thoroughly, dry, and break into bite-size pieces
into a salad bowl. Sprinkle with the chopped eggs and bacon.
Toss with Yogurt Dressing or French Dressing.

## PENNSYLVANIA DUTCH WILTED LETTUCE
### (4 servings)

4 slices bacon
⅓ cup sugar
½ teaspoon salt
½ cup vinegar
2 hard boiled eggs
Soft lettuce and/or young dandelion greens

Dice the bacon and fry until crisp. Remove and set aside. Add the
sugar, salt, and vinegar to the bacon drippings and add ¼ cup
water. When this comes to a boil, pour over the greens, which
have been broken into pieces, and toss. Sprinkle coarsely chopped
eggs and diced or crumbled bacon over the top and toss.

# Platter Salads

Every salad on a platter is a thing of beauty. It is "a joy forever" to dieters, pickers, and omnivorous eaters alike, because the various ingredients are presented attractively arranged for the guest to choose what he enjoys, what he needs, or—alas—what he is allowed to eat.

Here is where you can let your creativity run rampant, designing an abstraction on a platter, massing color and form with piles of cucumbers, string beans, or beets, ranks of asparagus or hearts of palm, chubby stuffed tomatoes, and stuffed artichokes rising over all.

Did you ever try making a miniature smorgasbord spread on a platter? Add to your handsome vegetable assortment several fish items, such as herring in sour cream or wine sauce, anchovies, sardines, or flaked cooked fish, as well as cold cuts and perhaps a chicken salad. This impressive presentation looks as if you had spent all day working your fingers to the bone, but really there is nothing easier than to assemble these delicious ingredients into a dainty dish to set before a guest. It is necessary to arrange the various items with space or a little lettuce between so they will not run or merge into each other. Watch the color scheme too, not potato salad right next to a white fish nor tomatoes or beets next to a red meat. This kind of a salad is especially suitable for a supper following an evening event, because it can be put together early, and produced still in its prime when the party is ready for it.

### VEGETABLE SALAD PLATTER
(8 *servings*)

1 large head Boston lettuce
½ pound zucchini, sliced
2 kohlrabi or white turnips, sliced very thin

1  head cauliflower, pulled into sprigs
1  head celery, sliced
4  scallions, chopped
1  bunch carrots, cut into strips
1  box cherry tomatoes or 3 tomatoes cut into wedges
2  green peppers, sliced
1  bunch water cress or parsley
½  cup French Dressing* or Vinaigrette*

Wash, dry, and pull the lettuce apart, do not break it up. Line the platter with lettuce, cup face up. Prepare all of the vegetables. To assemble the salad, arrange the vegetables on the lettuce in piles by color—putting contrasting ones next to each other, placing the white cauliflower and pale greens to offset the bright carrots and tomatoes. Use the water cress or parsley when you need to fill in a spot of darker green, and around the edge here and there. Pour the dressing over at the last minute.

## SALAD PLATTER
### (4 servings)

½  pound cold sliced ham
½  cup diced celery
1  cup seedless white grapes
¼  cup French Dressing*
4  tomatoes, peeled and quartered
1  teaspoon basil
½  teaspoon sugar

Arrange the ham on sides of the platter in slices or roll-ups. Mix the celery with grapes and moisten with a little dressing. Sprinkle the tomatoes with basil and sugar. Make separate piles of the tomatoes and the grapes mixed with celery. Sprinkle a little dressing over all.

# Chef's Salads

All of these mixed salads go equally well before, with, or after the main course. By adding to a tossed green salad julienne strips of meat, cheese, and/or fish, you can make it into a meal as the very popular "Chef's Salad."

Anything goes in a chef's salad. You may be using up what's in the refrigerator, the last few slices of cheese, the steak left from dinner or the bacon from breakfast. You may be planning a high-style luncheon party. The classic version of the chef's *chef d'oeuvre* would be a bowlful of green salad generously heaped with shredded ham, chicken, and Swiss cheese. Other smoked and fresh meats, other firm cheeses, a few croutons, would blend together equally well. Shrimp on top makes a different salad and a different chef out of you.

### BASIC CHEF'S SALAD
### (6 servings)

1 head lettuce
Escarole, endive, garden lettuce, water cress, or young spinach
2 tomatoes, peeled and cubed
1 cucumber, peeled and cubed
3 scallions, minced
½ pound ham, tongue and/or chicken, cut into julienne strips
¼ pound Swiss or Cheddar cheese, cut into julienne strips
1 can anchovies, drained
¾ cup French Dressing*

Tear up the lettuce and use an equal amount of other greens, one or a mixture. Put into a large shallow salad bowl. Add the tomatoes, cucumber, and scallions. Scatter the meat, cheese, and anchovies on top and pour the dressing over. Toss at table.

## CHEF'S SALAD BOWL
### (6 servings)

2 heads Boston lettuce
1 cup julienne strips cooked chicken
1 cup sliced radishes
1 cup julienne strips baked ham
1 cup julienne strips Swiss cheese
1 cucumber
½ bunch water cress
2 tomatoes
¼ cup French Dressing*

Tear up the lettuce and put into a salad bowl. Add chicken, sliced radishes, ham strips, cheese, and peeled and sliced cucumber. Place peeled tomato wedges around the rim and tuck in the water cress. Add French Dressing. Toss at table.

## CHEF'S SALAD
### (4 servings)

1 head soft lettuce
1 cup julienne strips cooked chicken
½ cup julienne strips celery
1 cup julienne strips Swiss cheese
2 tomatoes, peeled and quartered
1 (4 ounce) can artichoke hearts
2 hard boiled eggs, quartered
¼ cup Thousand Island Dressing*
¼ cup French Dressing*

Tear the lettuce into bite-size pieces and toss with the remaining ingredients except the eggs. Garnish with eggs and pour over a mixture of the two dressings. Toss at table. You may prefer to arrange the ingredients in piles on the greens and toss all at table.

### SHRIMP CHEF'S SALAD
(*4 servings*)

1 quart mixed greens, torn into small pieces
½ pound cooked shrimp
2 tablespoons capers
¼ cup Lemon French Dressing*
Curry powder (optional)

Put the chilled greens in a bowl. If the shrimp are small, leave them whole; if medium, slice them through the center lengthwise; if large, slice them through the center and then cut across, making each shrimp into four pieces. Place on top of greens and sprinkle with capers. Pour over the dressing, to which you have added a little curry powder, if you wish.

### SALMON CHEF'S SALAD
(*4 servings*)

1 (7¾ ounce) can salmon
1 cucumber, peeled and diced
1 large tomato, peeled and chopped
3 tablespoons French Dressing*
1 teaspoon lemon juice
3 tablespoons sour cream
1 tablespoon chopped fresh dill or 1 teaspoon dry

Flake the salmon and combine with cucumber and tomato. Mix the French Dressing with lemon juice, sour cream, and dill, and blend with the salmon mixture.

## DEVILED EGG CHEF'S SALAD
### (6–8 servings)

6 hard boiled eggs
¼ teaspoon minced chives or 1 teaspoon minced scallions
2 tablespoons butter or oil
2 tablespoons Mayonnaise*
⅛ teaspoon curry powder
½ teaspoon salt
¼ teaspoon pepper
1 head soft lettuce
1 head chicory, romaine, or leaf lettuce
3–4 tomatoes
2 cucumbers
1 cup shredded salami, baloney, or other sausage
1 can anchovies
½ cup Garlic French Dressing*

Cut the eggs in half and remove yolks. Sauté the chives or scallions in the butter or oil for 2 minutes, then add to the mashed egg yolks with the Mayonnaise, curry, salt, and pepper. Fill the egg whites with the yolk mixture. Tear the greens and put into a salad bowl. Peel and slice tomatoes and cucumbers and arrange the vegetables on the lettuce. Add salami or other sausage. Add the oil as well as the anchovies. Toss with the dressing. Then add the stuffed eggs around the edge of the salad.

Salad-happy Californians dreamed up Caesar Salad, and it has caught the public fancy. Here is my special version of this magnificent salad bowl.

## CAESAR SALAD
### (6 servings)

1 clove garlic, crushed
¾ cup olive or salad oil
2 quarts salad greens: head lettuce, water cress, leaf lettuce, endive, etc.
1 teaspoon Worcestershire sauce
1 teaspoon salt
¼ teaspoon freshly ground pepper
1 egg, coddled
¼ cup lemon juice
3 ounces Roquefort cheese, crumbled
2 cups croutons, toasted or fried

Add the garlic to the ¾ cup of salad oil or olive oil and let stand several hours. Tear the salad greens into bite-size pieces using assorted greens. Put into a large bowl with the oil and the seasonings. Open the egg (cooked for 1 minute only) onto the greens. Sprinkle with the lemon juice and toss until all greens are coated with the oil and seasonings. Add cheese and toss again. Top with croutons.

## CALIFORNIA CAESAR SALAD
### (8 servings)

1 head lettuce
1 head romaine
2 eggs, coddled
6 anchovies, chopped
½ teaspoon freshly ground pepper
1 tablespoon Worcestershire sauce
½ teaspoon prepared mustard

¼  cup grated Parmesan cheese
½  cup French Dressing*
1  cup garlic croutons

Wash the lettuce and dry thoroughly. Break up into a large bowl. Open the eggs (cooked 1 minute only) into a bowl and add remaining ingredients except croutons. Mix thoroughly and pour over the greens. Add croutons and toss.

# Vegetable Salads

Cooked vegetable salad is an ideal buffet dish, because it needs no cutting on the plate, and can be eaten unimpeded from the lap. Having no juice to slop around, it goes well with other comestibles on your one plate. It can be made ready ahead, and waits without wilting. Substantial and colorful, it fills the place of both a vegetable and a salad.

### COOKED VEGETABLE SALAD
#### (8–10 servings)

1 package frozen peas
1 package frozen cut green beans
1 package frozen baby limas
1 package frozen corn
1 cup diced cooked celery
1½ cups diced cooked carrots
½ cup French Dressing* or ½ cup Mayonnaise*
¼ cup cream (optional)

Cook the vegetables according to package instructions, drain and chill. Mix together with the celery and carrots, which have been chilled. Toss gently with French Dressing—don't use too much, the salad should not be wet, just moistened. If you use Mayonnaise, thin with cream or juice from the vegetables.

### THREE OR FOUR BEAN SALAD
#### (8 servings)

1 pound green beans or 1 box frozen
1 pound wax beans or 1 box frozen
1 box frozen small limas
1 (1-pound) can kidney beans

3 scallions, chopped
1 clove garlic, crushed
½ cup French Dressing*
Salad greens (optional)

Cut and cook the green and wax beans if using fresh. If frozen buy cut or French cut and cook all the package beans according to directions. Toss all of the beans together with the scallions. Mix garlic with the dressing, and pour over. Toss again. Serve on greens if you wish.

### BEAN AND ASPARAGUS SALAD WITH GRAPES
(4–6 servings)

½ pound green beans, or 1 box whole frozen beans
1 pound asparagus, or 2 boxes frozen, or 1 can white, drained
¾–1 pound white grapes
1 head iceberg, Boston, or leaf lettuce
Juice 1 lemon
2 tablespoons oil
½ cup heavy cream
½ teaspoon salt
⅛ teaspoon pepper
¼ teaspoon sugar

Cook the beans in salted water until just tender; rinse them at once in cold water so they will not be overdone. If using fresh asparagus, tie it in 4–5 bunches, removing about half of each stem, and cook in a quart of salted water. Remove from water as soon as it is almost tender. If using frozen, follow package directions, cooking a little less than prescribed. Refrigerate the vegetables. Pull the grapes off the stems. Break the greens into bite-size pieces in a salad bowl. Place the asparagus and beans on the greens. Garnish with grapes. Pour over the dressing made by mixing all remaining ingredients together thoroughly.

## ASPARAGUS VINAIGRETTE
### (6 servings)

2½ pounds fresh asparagus, or 2 cans large white asparagus
¾ cup Vinaigrette*
Greens (optional)

Cook the asparagus, being careful not to overcook. Drain and cool. Marinate in the dressing for about an hour. If you use canned asparagus, drain thoroughly. Serve on lettuce if you wish.

## BEETROOT SALAD
### (6 servings)

4–6 large beets, cooked
1 onion, sliced thin
½ cup Mayonnaise*
2 teaspoons tarragon vinegar
¼ cup heavy cream, whipped

Slice the beets, and add the onion, and mix in a salad bowl. Mix the Mayonnaise with the vinegar, and fold in the whipped cream. Pour the sauce over the salad. Serve cold.

## ROMAINE AND BEET SALAD
### (4 servings)

1 head romaine lettuce
2 cups julienne of beets
3 ounces Roquefort or blue cheese (optional)
¼ cup French Dressing*

Pull off most of the large leaves of the romaine and break them into bite-size pieces. Pull inside leaves apart leaving them whole. Put the torn-up pieces in a bowl and mix with the beets. Garnish with the center leaves, sprinkle with crumbled cheese if you wish. Add the French Dressing.

## BEET AND FRUIT SALAD
### (6 servings)

½  pound sliced cooked beets
1  cup cubed pineapple
1  apple, peeled, cored, and sliced
Sections of 2 oranges
2  bananas, sliced
½  cup Lemon French Dressing*
½  cup coarsely chopped peanuts

Mix the beets with the fruit, working quickly so that the apples
and bananas will not darken. Pour the Lemon French Dressing
over and sprinkle peanuts over the top.

## CAULIFLOWER SALAD
### (6 servings)

1  large head cauliflower
Salad greens
2  tomatoes
1  green pepper
½  cup Mayonnaise*
1  tablespoon lemon juice
1–2  tablespoons minced chives and/or parsley

Cook the cauliflower in salted water until it starts to get tender,
about 10–15 minutes. Do not overcook or it will be mushy and
will fall apart. Drain and chill. Place on some salad greens on a
deep platter or shallow salad bowl. Peel and slice or cut the tomatoes in eighths and put around the cauliflower. Cut the green
pepper into strips and put around the salad. Mix the Mayonnaise
with lemon juice. Spread a thin layer on the cauliflower and a
little on the tomatoes. Sprinkle chives and/or parsley over all.

## CAULIFLOWER AND AVOCADO SALAD
(6 *servings*)

1 large head cauliflower
¼ cup vinegar
6 tablespoons oil
1½ teaspoons salt
¼ teaspoon pepper
3 avocados
½ cup coarsely ground almonds
1 small onion, minced
Dash of nutmeg
Tomato wedges, radishes, olives (garnish)

Cook the cauliflower in salted water until tender. Mix half of the oil and vinegar with 1 teaspoon salt and the pepper and pour over the cauliflower while it is still warm. Chill. Peel and mash the avocados and mix with remaining oil, vinegar, salt, almonds, and onion. Add nutmeg and any remaining marinade from the cauliflower. Put the cold cauliflower on a round plate. Pour the avocado sauce over. Garnish if you wish with tomato wedges, and/or radishes, and olives.

## CELERY VICTOR
(8 *servings*)

8 celery hearts or 4 heads pascal celery
Beef broth, consommé, or bouillon cubes
Water cress or salad greens
1 cup French Dressing* or Vináigrette*

Cook the celery in broth, consommé, or water with bouillon cubes until just tender. If using large stalks, remove outside leaves and cut the head in half before cooking. Let celery cool in the broth. Be sure to remove from heat before the celery is done as it will continue to cook in the hot broth. Chill. Serve on a bed of water cress or salad greens and spoon the dressing over.

## CELERY ROOT SALAD
### (6 *servings*)

1 pound celery root
½ cup French Dressing*

Scrub the roots. Boil in salted water until tender. Plunge into very cold water and then peel and slice very thin into a bowl. Pour the French Dressing over and let marinate for a couple of hours.

## CHICK PEA SALAD
### (4 *servings*)

2 cups drained canned garbanzo peas
½ pound cream cheese, diced
2 onions, sliced thin
½ cup olive oil
¼ cup lemon juice
1 teaspoon salt
¼ teaspoon pepper
½ teaspoon ground coriander
Salad greens

Combine the peas, cheese, and onions. Mix the rest of the ingredients, except greens, and pour over the pea mixture. Let stand several hours before serving. Toss, and serve on lettuce or other greens.

## WINTER SALAD
### (6 servings)

2 large Bermuda or Spanish onions
1 cup milk
1 head celery or 3 celery hearts
2 large cooked beets
2 hard boiled eggs
1 teaspoon mustard
1 teaspoon salt
¼ teaspoon pepper
½ teaspoon sugar
1 teaspoon anchovy paste (optional)
¼ cup olive oil
2 tablespoons wine vinegar

Boil the onions in half milk and half water until tender. Drain and chill. Slice the celery and beets, and chill while making the dressing. Chop the eggs and mix with mustard, salt, pepper, and sugar. Add the anchovy paste if you wish. Stir in the oil, blending well, and then the vinegar. Mix the sliced onions with celery and beets, and pour the dressing over. Let stand several hours in the refrigerator.

French or globe artichokes are an artistic addition to a meal as well as a taste delight. These artichokes must be cooked, drained, and chilled. Trim the stem so the artichoke will sit flat on a plate. Cut the leaves across the top or trim each leaf with scissors if you wish. Boil in a large pot of water with 1 tablespoon salt and 1 tablespoon vinegar to the quart. The artichoke is done when a leaf pulls out easily—30–45 minutes depending upon size. Drain upside down.

You can buy tiny artichoke hearts in cans or in jars or frozen. Any variety is a good addition to a mixed salad. The best of the canned artichokes are the *fonds* or bottoms. They're expensive, but oh so good!

## ARTICHOKES
### (4 *servings*)

4 Artichokes*
½–1 cup Vinaigrette* or ⅓ cup Mayonnaise*
1–1½ tablespoons prepared mustard or 1 cube butter, melted

Cook the Artichokes. Chill and serve on a plate and pass the Vinaigrette or Mayonnaise mixed with mustard, or serve hot with hot drawn butter.

## ARTICHOKES IN MUSTARD SAUCE
### (6 *servings*)

12 tiny artichokes
2 cloves garlic
Juice 1 lemon
½ cup French Dressing*
¼ cup prepared brown mustard

Pull off the outside leaves of the artichokes and clip the tips of the rest of the leaves if you wish. Boil in salt water with the garlic and lemon juice until tender. You may test it by pulling out a leaf. If it pulls out easily, the artichokes are done. Drain upside down. Marinate for several hours in the dressing made by blending the French Dressing and mustard.

# Raw Vegetable Salads

There are many vegetables which, though usually served cooked, are great raw, such as mushrooms, zucchini, carrots, cauliflower, and asparagus. They are available for salads in addition to the ones often eaten raw, such as celery, radishes, onions, fennel, cucumbers, and avocados.

## AVOCADOS
### (4 servings)

2 avocados
Juice ½ lemon
¼ cup Lemon French Dressing*
Lettuce

Cut the avocados in half and remove pits. Sprinkle edges with lemon juice to prevent discoloration. Fill center with Lemon French Dressing and serve on a bed of lettuce.

## AVOCADO SALAD
### (6 servings)

2 cups peeled diced avocado
2 hard boiled eggs, coarsely chopped
3 medium tomatoes, peeled and diced
1 teaspoon grated onion
1 teaspoon lemon juice
¼ teaspoon salt
Dash of freshly ground pepper
½ teaspoon sugar
About ¼ cup French Dressing* or Lemon French Dressing*
Lettuce

Combine the avocado, eggs, tomatoes, onion, and seasonings. Add enough French Dressing to moisten and toss until well blended. Serve on lettuce.


## FILLED AVOCADO SALAD
### (6 servings)

½ cup oil
¼ cup wine vinegar
1 teaspoon salt
¼ teaspoon freshly ground pepper
½ teaspoon paprika
3 scallions
2 tomatoes
1 clove garlic, crushed
3 avocados

Mix the oil, vinegar, salt, pepper, and paprika. Chop the scallions, peel and chop the tomatoes, and mix together with the garlic. Add to the dressing. Cut the avocados in half lengthwise and remove pits. Fill centers at once with the dressing mixture.


## AVOCADO CITRUS SALAD
### (6 servings)

1 head lettuce
2 avocados
1 cup grapefruit sections
1 cup orange sections
⅓ cup Lemon French Dressing*

Line a salad bowl with lettuce. Tear the remaining lettuce into bite-size pieces. Peel and slice the avocados into the bowl. Add the Lemon French Dressing and toss together lightly.

## CUCUMBERS IN SOUR CREAM
### (6 servings)

3–4 cucumbers
2 tablespoons salt
1–1½ cups sour cream
1 tablespoon sugar
3 tablespoons vinegar
½ teaspoon freshly ground pepper
1 tablespoon minced dill or chives (optional)

Slice the cucumbers thin. Sprinkle generously with salt and let stand for at least a couple of hours. Rinse in cold water and squeeze out the moisture. Mix rest of ingredients, and fold the cucumbers into the sauce. Chill.


## SHREDDED CUCUMBER SALAD
### (4 servings)

2 large cucumbers
2 tablespoons salt
1 tablespoon peanut oil
1 tablespoon soy sauce
1 tablespoon sesame oil
1 teaspoon MSG
1 clove garlic, crushed
½ teaspoon sugar
¼ teaspoon pepper

Peel and shred the cucumbers and sprinkle with salt. Let stand in the refrigerator for several hours. Rinse in a sieve under cold running water. Drain thoroughly, and squeeze out moisture. Mix all of the remaining ingredients together, and pour over the cucumbers.

## GRATED CUCUMBER SALAD
### (4 servings)

2 cucumbers, grated
2 tablespoons grated onion
1 teaspoon salt
¼ teaspoon pepper
1 cup yogurt

Drain the grated cucumbers. Combine all of the ingredients.

## STUFFED CUCUMBER SALAD
### (6 servings)

3 cucumbers, cut in half lengthwise
6 tablespoons cottage cheese
2 tablespoons minced celery
2 tablespoons minced green onion
1 teaspoon salt
2 tablespoons Mayonnaise*
Chives (garnish)

Scrape the seeds from the center of the cucumber, and mix with
the remaining ingredients, except chives. Taste for seasoning and
refill the cucumbers. Serve on the half shell chilled or put halves
together and chill for several hours and then cut into thick slices.
Sprinkle with chives.

## HAWAIIAN CUCUMBER SHOYU SALAD
### (4 servings)

¼ pound very fresh white fish, raw
⅓ cup vinegar
1 teaspoon minced ginger
2 tablespoons sugar
½ teaspoon salt
2 cucumbers, sliced
1½ tablespoons Shoyu, or soy sauce

Cut the fish in very thin pieces. Mix the vinegar, ginger, sugar, and salt, and pour over the fish. Let stand half an hour. Add cucumbers, which have been let stand in salt, rinsed, and drained. Add Shoyu sauce or soy sauce, and mix gently.

## COLE SLAW
### (6–8 servings)

½ teaspoon salt
½ teaspoon onion salt
¼ teaspoon pepper
1 tablespoon sugar
1 teaspoon mustard
1 teaspoon celery seed or ½ teaspoon celery salt
3 tablespoons wine vinegar
½ cup olive oil
4 cups shredded cabbage
1 sweet bell pepper, red or green, chopped
1 tablespoon minced parsley

Blend all of the seasonings with the vinegar and oil in a large bowl. Add cabbage and the red or green pepper and mix thoroughly. Just before serving, sprinkle with the minced parsley.

## SOUR CREAM COLE SLAW
### (4 servings)

1 small head cabbage
1 cup sour cream
1 tablespoon vinegar
1 tablespoon sugar
1 teaspoon salt
½ teaspoon pepper
½ teaspoon prepared mustard (optional)

Shred the cabbage fine. Mix the sour cream with vinegar, sugar, salt, and pepper. Add mustard if you wish. Fold into the cabbage, mixing thoroughly. Let stand a few hours before serving.

## FINOCCHIO SALAD
(8 *servings*)

1  head soft lettuce
3  cups diced finocchio
1  clove garlic, crushed, or ½ teaspoon garlic salt or powder
4  tomatoes
¼  cup French Dressing*

Wash and tear the lettuce into bite-size pieces, dry and chill. Soak the finocchio in ice water with garlic. When ready to put the salad together, drain the finocchio, peel and quarter the tomatoes, and arrange both on salad greens in a bowl. Pour the dressing over.

## LEEK SALAD
(6 *servings*)

3 or 4 young tender leeks
2–3  tomatoes, peeled
½  teaspoon dry tarragon or 1 teaspoon fresh
1  teaspoon dry basil or 1 tablespoon fresh
Soft lettuce or romaine
¼  cup garlic croutons
¼  cup French Dressing*

The number of leeks and tomatoes depends upon their size. Cut the leeks into pieces about ½ inch long. Cut the tomatoes into sections and mix the two gently. Sprinkle with the herbs. Line a salad bowl with soft lettuce or romaine. Add croutons to the leeks and fold in the French Dressing. Put into the greens and serve at once.

## MUSHROOM CELERY SALAD
### (6 servings)

¾ pound mushrooms
1 head celery
½ cup olive oil
⅛ cup lemon juice
1 teaspoon salt
¼ teaspoon pepper
Bibb or Boston lettuce

Wipe the mushrooms and remove stems (use stems for soup or sauce, do not throw away). If the mushrooms are not pure white, peel the caps. Slice thin across the head making half oval slices. Wash the celery, pull the stalk apart, and cut across making slices the width of the mushrooms. They will be similar in shape. Mix together. Blend the oil, lemon juice, salt, and pepper, and toss gently into the salad. Chill and serve on the lettuce.

## HEARTS OF PALM SALAD
### (6-8 servings)

1 (14 ounce) can hearts of palm
Shredded lettuce
¼ cup Lemon French Dressing*
Freshly ground pepper

Cut the larger pieces of palm in half or quarters lengthwise. Place on the lettuce and add the dressing. Dust top with a little pepper.

## PALM AND TOMATO SALAD
### (8 servings)

1 head chicory lettuce, shredded
1 (14 ounce) can hearts of palm
2 tomatoes
½ cup French Dressing*
1 teaspoon lemon juice

Put the crisp lettuce on a platter or individual plates. Put the pieces of palm on the lettuce and garnish with tomatoes. Pour over the dressing, which has been mixed with lemon juice.

## TOMATO SALAD
### (8 servings)

4 large tomatoes
1 teaspoon thyme
½ teaspoon salt
¼ teaspoon sugar
½ teaspoon pepper
2 tablespoons olive oil
2 tablespoons minced chives or scallions (optional)

Peel and slice the tomatoes and arrange them in overlapping rows around a serving dish. Sprinkle with thyme, salt, sugar, and olive oil, and let stand for an hour or two. You may add the chives or scallions if you wish. You may cut the tomatoes in eighths if you prefer.

## TOMATO AND AVOCADO SALAD
### (6 servings)

3 tomatoes, peeled, cut in wedges
1 large avocado, peeled, sliced
½ cup French Dressing*
1 head lettuce
2 tablespoons grated cheese

Marinate the tomatoes and avocado in the French Dressing in the refrigerator. Tear the lettuce into bite-size pieces into the salad bowl. Add the marinated tomatoes and avocado. Sprinkle with the cheese and toss lightly.

### STUFFED TOMATOES
#### (4 *servings*)

4 large tomatoes
1 cup diced celery
1–2 tablespoons minced chives or scallions
2 teaspoons minced fresh dill or ½ teaspoon dried or same
quantity sweet basil
¾ cup Mayonnaise*
Lettuce

Cut the top off of the tomatoes and scoop out pulp and seeds. Mix the pulp, not much juice, with celery, chives or scallions, and dill or basil. Stir in the ½ cup Mayonnaise. If too thick, add a little of the tomato juice. Adjust seasoning to taste, adding salt, pepper, or lemon juice to taste. Refill tomatoes with the mixture. Chill, and serve on lettuce leaves. Top each with a generous dab of Mayonnaise.

## HAWAIIAN STUFFED TOMATO SALAD
### (6 *servings*)

6 tomatoes
1½ cups shredded pineapple
½ cup chopped roasted peanuts
2 tablespoons Lemon French Dressing*
1 teaspoon salt
Lettuce

Peel the tomatoes and cut slice from top, and remove seeds and pulp. Chill the tomatoes. Combine tomato pulp, pineapple, peanuts, Lemon French Dressing, and salt. Fill tomatoes with the mixture, and serve on lettuce leaves.

## ZUCCHINI SALAD WITH VEGETABLES
### (8 *servings*)

8 zucchini
2 tomatoes, peeled and coarsely chopped
1 green pepper, chopped
1 onion, chopped fine
1 teaspoon sugar
1 teaspoon salt
½ teaspoon pepper
¼ teaspoon paprika
2–4 tablespoons Mayonnaise* or French Dressing*
Lettuce

Cut the zucchini in thin slices, do not peel. Mix with all of the other ingredients. Add the dressing a tablespoon at a time. You do not want the salad to be too moist. Serve on lettuce.

## ZUCCHINI SALAD
### (6 servings)

6 small zucchini
1 tablespoon salt
Lettuce
¼ cup French Dressing*

Cook the zucchini with skin left on in salt water until almost tender, about 5 minutes. When cool, slice thin lengthwise in about ⅓ inch slices within 1 inch of the bottom and not through the skin. Spread gently apart fan shape. Put on lettuce and pour the dressing over.

Potato salad is the king of the heavy salads in many lands: *Kartoffelsalat* in Germany, *Papas a la Huancaina* in Peru, *Salatt El Bataater* in Lebanon, and what would we do without our potato salad with the cold ham at supper? Under any name, this dish is best made of new potatoes, if available; they're less mushy. You may vary potato salad tremendously by making it with French Dressing, Cooked Dressing, Sour Cream Dressing or with Mayonnaise.

## POTATO SALAD
### (4–6 servings)

2 pounds potatoes, boiled in jackets
6 tablespoons olive oil
6 tablespoons wine vinegar
½ cup beef broth
1 teaspoon salt
¼ teaspoon pepper
1 small onion, minced, or 2 tablespoons minced scallions
1 tablespoon minced parsley

Peel and slice the potatoes while warm. Pour a mixture of oil, vinegar, and broth over the potatoes while they are still warm. Let stand for 1 hour. Mix the salt, pepper, onions, and parsley, and fold into salad.

## POTATO SALAD WITH MAYONNAISE
### (4-6 servings)

- 2 pounds potatoes, boiled in jackets
- 1 onion, sliced thin
- 3 tablespoons minced parsley
- 1 cup Mayonnaise*

Peel and slice the potatoes. Mix gently with the onion. Add 2 tablespoons of parsley to the Mayonnaise, and fold it into the potato salad. Garnish the top with remaining minced parsley.

# Poultry and Meat Salads

Meat salads often make the meal. They are delightful as a luncheon or supper dish, especially in hot weather. Served in small portions they are used as an appetizer salad. Leftovers come into the salad bowl with success. Turkey, chicken, ham, beef, veal, or what you have, combined with something crisp and a tangy dressing make a tasty salad.

## CHICKEN SALAD WITH ALMONDS
### (4 servings)

2 cups diced cooked chicken
1 cup chopped celery
¾ cup sliced toasted almonds
1 tablespoon minced parsley
1 cup Mayonnaise*
¼ cup chicken stock
Lettuce

Mix the chicken, celery, almonds, and parsley. Combine the Mayonnaise and chicken stock, and stir into the salad. Serve on lettuce.

## CHICKEN SALAD WITH CREAM DRESSING
### (6 servings)

1 quart cut up cooked chicken
1½ cups chopped celery
2 cups Mayonnaise*
½ cup strong chicken broth
½ cup heavy cream, whipped
2–3 tablespoons sliced truffles (optional)
Greens
Tomato wedges, hard boiled eggs, olives (optional garnishes)

Cut the chicken into large bite-size pieces, preferably about 1 inch long. Mix with celery and Mayonnaise. Combine broth and cream, and stir into the salad mixture. Fold in truffles if you wish. Serve on crisp greens. You may garnish with tomato wedges, hard boiled eggs, and/or olives.

## CHICKEN AND CORN SALAD
### (8 servings)

3 cups diced cooked chicken
2 cups cooked, canned, or frozen corn
4 tomatoes, peeled and cubed
2 green peppers, chopped
2 cups Mayonnaise*
Lettuce

Mix the chicken and corn with the tomatoes and peppers. Stir in 1½ cups of Mayonnaise, and adjust the seasoning to taste. Serve on a bed of lettuce, and decorate with remaining Mayonnaise.

## CHICKEN SALAD MOLD
### (6 servings)

2 cups diced cooked chicken
1 cup chopped celery
1 cup white grapes, cut in halves
2 tablespoons minced parsley
1 teaspoon salt
¼ teaspoon white pepper
1½ tablespoons gelatin
½ cup hot chicken stock
1 cup Mayonnaise*
2 tablespoons heavy cream

Mix the chicken, celery, grapes, and parsley. Season with salt and pepper. Soften the gelatin in ¼ cup cold water, and dissolve in the hot chicken stock, and stir into the salad. Combine the Mayonnaise with cream, and fold in. Put into a wet mold or in 6 individual molds.

## CHICKEN LIVER SALAD
### (6 *servings*)

½ pound chicken livers
2 tablespoons butter
½ teaspoon salt
¼ teaspoon freshly ground pepper
1 head lettuce
½ bunch curly endive (optional)
4 scallions, chopped
¼ cup crumbled Roquefort or blue cheese
2 hard boiled eggs, chopped
⅓ cup French Dressing*

Sauté the chicken livers in the butter with salt and pepper until lightly browned. Chill. Drain and cut into small pieces. Tear the lettuce into bite-size pieces. Add the chicken livers, scallions, cheese, and eggs. Toss with French Dressing.

## TURKEY SALAD
### (8 *servings*)

3 cups bite-size pieces roast turkey
2 cups diced celery
2 cups white seedless grapes (optional)
½ cup sliced blanched almonds (optional)
1 tablespoon grated onion
¼ cup strong turkey broth, if available
¼ cup French Dressing* (optional)
¾ cup Mayonnaise*
Greens
2 hard boiled eggs (optional)

Mix the turkey and celery and add if you wish the grapes and/or nuts. Mix the onion with strong turkey broth, or French Dressing, and the Mayonnaise. Toss the salad with the dressing and refrigerate for several hours. Serve on a bed of greens and garnish with a few nuts and grapes or sliced or quartered eggs.

### SUNSET SALAD
#### (4 servings)

1½  cups young cabbage, shredded
1½  cups julienne strips smoked cooked tongue
1½  cups julienne strips cooked chicken
½  cup Lorenzo Dressing*

Mix the cabbage, tongue, and chicken. You should have about the same quantity of each. Top with the dressing and toss lightly but thoroughly.

### COBB SALAD
#### (6 servings)

1  head soft lettuce
½  bunch water cress
2  large tomatoes, peeled and diced
2  cups diced cooked chicken
2  avocados, peeled and diced
4  slices bacon cooked
2  tablespoons chopped scallions
4  ounces Roquefort cheese
2  hard boiled eggs, minced or grated
Minced parsley or chives (garnish)
½  cup French Dressing*

Use lettuce such as Boston, leaf, or chicory. Wash, dry thoroughly, and shred. Cut up the water cress. Line a flat salad bowl with greens. Put the tomatoes, chicken, and avocados in three separate strips across the bowl. Crumble crisp bacon over the salad. Add the scallions, the grated or crumbled Roquefort cheese, and eggs; top with minced parsley or chives. Add the dressing and toss at table.

### SWEETBREAD SALAD
### (6 *servings*)

4 pairs sweetbreads
1 tablespoon lemon juice
1 tablespoon salt
½ envelope gelatin
¼ cup white wine
1 cup Mayonnaise*
1 tablespoon minced parsley
1 teaspoon minced chives (optional)
Salad greens

Cook the sweetbreads in water to cover to which you have added the lemon juice and salt. Simmer for 15–20 minutes. Drain and put in ice water for an hour or more. Sprinkle the gelatin on ¼ cup cold water and dissolve over heat. When cool, add the white wine and fold into the Mayonnaise. Add the parsley, and chives if you wish. Mix well. Cut the sweetbreads into small bite-size pieces removing any membrane. Pour the Mayonnaise over the sweetbreads. Chill for several hours. Serve on lettuce.

### BEEF SALAD
### (4 *servings*)

2 cups diced cooked roast beef
1 cup diced celery
1 tablespoon chopped chives or scallions
½ cup Mayonnaise*
1 tablespoon vinegar
1 teaspoon prepared mustard
Lettuce
1 teaspoon minced parsley

Mix the beef, celery, and chives. Combine the Mayonnaise with vinegar and mustard and toss into the salad. Serve on lettuce and sprinkle with parsley.

## HAM SALAD
### (4 *servings*)

2 cups ham, julienne strips or diced
1 cup celery, diced or julienne strips
2 small sweet pickles, chopped
2 hard boiled eggs, quartered
1 tablespoon prepared mustard
1 teaspoon pickle juice
⅓ cup Mayonnaise*
Greens

Combine the ham with celery, pickles, and eggs. Mix the mustard and pickle juice into the Mayonnaise. Toss all together. Serve on a bed of greens.

# Fish Salads

The meat salad is not the only salad that makes a meal. Many another salad meal comes out of the sea. A fish salad is delicious for luncheon, supper, or an evening party, and substantial enough to rest on its own laurels (or a bed of lettuce). In addition to the usual—but delicious—salads of shrimp, crab, lobster, tuna, or salmon, fisherman's luck brings up the more exotic salad of mussels, or the marine mélange that makes a bouillabaisse salad. Like the typical Marseilles mixed fish bouillabaisse, this salad includes several kinds of fish and shellfish, presenting a handsome picture on the individual flat soup plate, or ranged on a deep platter in all the glory of its different colors, white fish, the pink of salmon, the red of shellfish, and the golden aura of saffron or curry.

### BOUILLABAISSE SALAD
### (8 servings)

½ pound each of two white fish such as cod and halibut
½ pound salmon
½ pound scallions (optional)
½ pound crabmeat
½ pound lobster meat
½ pound cooked shrimp
1 pound mussels or 12 oysters and/or clams (optional)
Greens, water cress or parsley (garnish)
2–3 lemons
Lemon French Dressing*

Poach the fish and scallions gently in a little salted water or preferably court bouillon for about 5 minutes. Reserve liquid and chill fish. When cold break the fish into large bite-size pieces. If using mussels steam in ¼ cup water or white wine until the shells open;

debeard and chill. Oysters and clams may be used raw. You do not have to have all of the different shellfishes; if lobster is not available or is terribly expensive double the quantity of shrimp or salmon; use your judgment and your fish monger to plan an effective, pretty salad. This salad is best assembled and served in individual flat soup plates, but you may use a large deep platter if you prefer. Place the white fish to offset the pink. Use firm lettuce leaves under the fish or garnish with water cress or parsley. Put a lemon wedge on each serving. Pass the dressing to which you have added 3 or 4 tablespoons of boiled down liquid from the fish.

### FISH SALAD
(6 *servings*)

- 2 pounds cooked fish, haddock, turbot, halibut, or cod
- 1 pound potatoes, cooked in their jackets
- 4 tomatoes
- 1 onion, sliced thin
- 2 tablespoons minced parsley
- ½ cup French Dressing*
- 1 tablespoon minced chives
- 1 tablespoon capers (optional)

Cook and bone the fish, and break into small bite-size pieces. Peel and slice the potatoes and tomatoes. Put alternate layers of fish, potatoes, tomatoes, onions, and a sprinkling of parsley in a bowl. Spoon a tablespoon or two of dressing on the layers. Top with remaining parsley and chives and dressing, and capers, if you wish. Let stand at least an hour in refrigerator.

## CRAB SALAD
### (4 servings)

2 cups crabmeat (1 pound)
1½ cups diced celery
2 teaspoons lemon juice
1 teaspoon Worcestershire sauce
¾ cup Mayonnaise*
4 large lettuce leaves
2 tomatoes
2 hard boiled eggs (garnish)

Use lump crabmeat or legs. Treat it gently so it doesn't get mashed. Mix with celery. Add lemon juice and Worcestershire sauce to the Mayonnaise, and fold into the crab. Serve on lettuce leaves and garnish with sections of tomato and hard boiled eggs.

## CRABMEAT SALAD WITH THOUSAND ISLAND DRESSING
### (4 servings)

1 pound crabmeat
Boston lettuce or other greens
2 tomatoes, and/or 1 avocado
Blanched almonds and/or capers
½–¾ cup Thousand Island Dressing*

Pick over the crabmeat trying not to break up the lumps. Put onto the greens in a bowl or individual plates. Garnish with sliced tomatoes and/or avocado, peeled and sliced. If you use the latter, sprinkle with lemon juice to prevent discoloration. Garnish with almonds and/or capers. Serve with Thousand Island Dressing or you may use a Caper Mayonnaise* or Mayonnaise with a half teaspoon of dill added.

## CRAB SALAD IN AVOCADOS

Make like Shrimp in Avocados*, substituting crabmeat for the shrimp.

## BASIC LOBSTER SALAD
### (4 servings)

1 pound cooked lobster meat
4 tablespoons olive oil
1 tablespoon wine vinegar
1 tablespoon lemon juice
½ teaspoon salt
¼ teaspoon white pepper
Lettuce cups or leaves
1 lemon (garnish)

Cut the lobster into large bite-size pieces. Mix the oil, vinegar, lemon juice, salt, and pepper. Shake to blend thoroughly. Put the lobster on lettuce and pour the dressing over. Garnish with lemon wedges.

## LOBSTER SALAD
### (6 servings)

1 pound cooked lobster meat
Juice ½ lemon
2 tablespoons sherry or white wine
⅔ cup diced celery
¼ cup Mayonnaise*
¼ cup heavy cream, whipped
Salad greens

Cut the lobster meat into bite-size pieces and moisten with lemon juice and wine. Let stand for about an hour. Add the celery. Mix the Mayonnaise with cream and fold into the salad. Blend thoroughly. Serve on greens.

## LOBSTER SALAD WITH MAYONNAISE
### (6 *servings*)

3 cups cut up cooked lobster meat
3 hard boiled eggs, chopped
½ cup diced celery
¼ cup minced parsley
1 tablespoon lemon juice
1 teaspoon Worcestershire sauce
1 teaspoon dry mustard
1 cup Mayonnaise*
Lettuce

Cut the lobster meat into large bite-size pieces. Put the eggs into a bowl, add celery and parsley and stir. Add lemon juice, Worcestershire sauce, and mustard to the Mayonnaise. Pour this over the eggs, add the lobster, and mix well. Serve on lettuce leaves.

## LOBSTER SALAD IN AVOCADOS

Make like Shrimp in Avocados*, substituting lobster meat for the shrimp.

## TO COOK SHRIMP

Start shrimp in cold water to cover, and when the water comes to a boil, remove from heat and let them cool in the water. If the shrimp are quite large let them boil for 3 or 4 minutes. Do not overcook or the shrimp will be dry. For more flavorful shrimp add the juice of one lemon and a teaspoon of freshly ground pepper for each quart of water, or cook the shrimp in any Court Bouillon*.

### SHRIMP SALAD
(4 *servings*)

1 pound small cooked shrimp
Juice ½ lemon
1 cup diced celery
1 cup chopped water cress or lettuce
3 tablespoons Mayonnaise*
1 tablespoon heavy cream
¼ teaspoon curry powder

Peel and devein the shrimp and sprinkle with lemon juice, and chill. Mix the shrimp with celery and water cress or lettuce. Mix the Mayonnaise with cream and curry powder to taste; add a teaspoon or two of the water the shrimp was cooked in. Moisten the salad carefully with the dressing.

### SHRIMP SALAD VINAIGRETTE
(6 *servings*)

2 pounds cooked shrimp or 3 cups canned or frozen
1 cup Vinaigrette*
½ teaspoon curry (optional)
Lettuce

If the shrimp are large, cut in half lengthwise; if very large, cut once more across. If using canned or frozen shrimp, drain them.

Put into a bowl and pour the Vinaigrette over. Add curry to the Vinaigrette if you wish. Let stand in refrigerator for at least two hours. Serve on lettuce leaves.

## SHRIMP WITH RED WINE
### (6 servings)

4 hard boiled egg yolks
1 teaspoon dry mustard
1 teaspoon anchovy paste
1 cup Mayonnaise*
½ cup red wine (claret type)
1 pound cooked shrimp
1 cup diced celery
2 tablespoons minced parsley
Lettuce

Mash the egg yolks with mustard and anchovy paste. Stir into the Mayonnaise. Add the wine and blend well. Fold in the shrimp, celery, and parsley. Chill. Serve in lettuce cups.

## SHRIMP IN AVOCADOS
### (6 servings)

3 avocados
1 lemon
1 pound cooked small shrimp
3 stalks celery, chopped
½ teaspoon celery salt
¾ cup Lemon French Dressing*
Lettuce

Cut the avocados in half lengthwise and remove pits, do not peel. Sprinkle avocados with lemon juice to prevent discoloration. Mix the shrimp, celery, and celery salt. Add ½ cup of the dressing. Put the avocados on lettuce leaves, fill with the shrimp mixture, and spoon the remaining dressing over.

## SOLE IN MARINADE
### (4 *servings*)

1 pound fillet of sole
¼ cup lemon juice
1½ cups olive oil
¾ teaspoon salt
⅛ teaspoon pepper

Cut the fish into strips about ½ inch wide and 1½ inches long. Place in a bowl and cover with lemon juice. Refrigerate for an hour or two turning the fish once or twice to coat all sides with the lemon juice. The lemon juice "cooks" the fish! Sprinkle with olive oil to which you have added the salt and pepper.

## COD OR FLOUNDER SALAD
### (6 *servings*)

2 cups flaked cooked fish
1 cup chopped celery
1 small onion, minced
1 cup diced cooked potatoes
8 sardines, drained and sliced
½ teaspoon salt
¼ teaspoon pepper
1 cup Mayonnaise*
1 tablespoon lemon juice
½ teaspoon dry thyme or dill
Lettuce
1 (½ ounce) can anchovy fillets
Celery leaves

Mix the fish gently with the vegetables and sardines. Sprinkle with salt and pepper. Mix the Mayonnaise with lemon juice and herbs. Toss the fish mixture very gently into the dressing. Serve on lettuce and decorate with anchovies and a few celery leaves.

## CANNED SALMON SALAD
### (6 servings)

1 cup diced cucumbers
1 cup diced celery
1 teaspoon minced onion
1 teaspoon minced parsley
1 (pound) can red salmon, drained
½ teaspoon salt
⅛ teaspoon pepper
2 teaspoons lemon juice
1 cup Mayonnaise*
Salad greens

Flake the salmon. Add the cucumbers, celery, onion, and parsley. Add the salt, pepper, and lemon juice to the Mayonnaise, and fold gently into the salmon mixture. Serve on greens.

## TUNA SALAD
### (8 servings)

2 (7 ounce) cans tuna
2 cups diced celery
2 teaspoons minced parsley (optional)
1 cup Mayonnaise*
Lettuce (optional)

Flake the tuna with the celery and parsley. Fold the Mayonnaise gently into the salad. Serve on lettuce if you wish.

## TUNA CHEESE SALAD
### (4 servings)

1 (7 ounce) can tuna
1 cup cubed Cheddar cheese
1 head lettuce, shredded
⅔ cup Mayonnaise*
Leaf lettuce

Drain, flake the tuna, combine with cheese and lettuce. Add the Mayonnaise, and toss. Serve in a bowl lined with lettuce.

## NICOISE SALAD
### (6 *servings*)

1 head Boston lettuce
½–¾ cup French Dressing*
2 cups French cut green beans, cooked
2 cups diced cooked potatoes
1 cup canned tuna
2–3 tomatoes, peeled and quartered
2 hard boiled eggs, quartered
6 anchovies, cut in half
1 tablespoon minced fresh tarragon, chervil, or parsley

Clean the lettuce and break into pieces, dry and put into a salad bowl. Sprinkle with a few tablespoons of the dressing. Arrange the beans, potatoes, and tuna on top of the greens, and place the tomatoes here and there around the edge. Decorate with eggs and anchovies. Pour over the remaining dressing and sprinkle with fresh tarragon, chervil, or parsley.

## MUSSELS REMOULADE
### (4 *servings*)

2 cups mussels, cooked or canned or frozen
¾ cup white wine or vermouth
Sprigs parsley
2 shallots or 3 scallions or 1 onion
½ cup Mayonnaise*
½ teaspoon anchovy paste
1 teaspoon minced pickles
½ teaspoon blended salad herbs
½–1 teaspoon capers

If you steam fresh mussels, you will need about 4 pounds. Scrub thoroughly and put in a large pot with the wine or vermouth, a few sprigs of parsley, and minced shallots, scallions, or onions. Cover tight, steam until the mussels open, about 5 minutes. Remove from shells. Reduce some of the liquid and use 2–3 tablespoons in the Mayonnaise. If using canned or frozen mussels add 2–3 tablespoons liquid in the Mayonnaise. Mix Mayonnaise with remaining ingredients and toss the mussels gently with the sauce.

## MUSSEL AND POTATO SALAD
### (6 servings)

4 pounds fresh mussels
1 onion
1 carrot
2 stalks celery
¾ cup white wine
5 medium potatoes, boiled in jackets
1 teaspoon tarragon or chervil
1 cup Mayonnaise*

Scrub and debeard the mussels and put them into a large pot with the onion, carrot, celery, and white wine. Steam until the shells open, about 5 minutes. Peel and slice the potatoes while hot. Sprinkle with ½ cup liquid from the mussels. Put alternate layers of mussels, reserving a few for garnish, and potatoes in a salad bowl. Mix the tarragon or chervil with the Mayonnaise. Spoon a little Mayonnaise on each layer. Cover with Mayonnaise and decorate with a few mussels.

## PASTA SALADS

Pasta makes a good, hearty salad, and can be served on any occasion when you might choose to serve a hot pasta. Macaroni salad teams well with cold cuts. In salad bowl or casserole, macaroni and cheese go well together.

## MACARONI CHEDDAR SALAD BOWL
### (6 servings)

2 cups cooked small elbow macaroni
2 tablespoons chopped onion
2 tablespoons chopped pimento
2 tablespoons chopped green pepper or dill pickles
½ cup diced celery
½ cup French Dressing*
¼ cup Mayonnaise*
1 cup shredded Cheddar cheese
1 teaspoon salt
¼ teaspoon pepper
Lettuce

Combine the macaroni, onion, pimento, green pepper or pickles, and celery, and let stand in the French Dressing for an hour or more. Add the Mayonnaise and cheese. Season with salt and pepper, and toss. Serve in a salad bowl lined with crisp lettuce.

## MACARONI SALAD PLATTER
### (6 servings)

1 (8 ounce) package small elbow macaroni
¼ cup French Dressing*
1 pound fresh peas shelled or 1 package frozen
1 can whole kernel corn or 1 package frozen
½ cup Mayonnaise*
½ cup sour cream
1 tablespoon prepared mustard
Lettuce

Cook the macaroni following package instructions. Drain. Put into a large bowl. Sprinkle with the French Dressing and toss. Stir in the peas and corn. If you use frozen, cook ahead and drain. Mix the Mayonnaise, sour cream, and mustard, and fold in the macaroni. Spoon into a 6 cup bowl or mold, and pack down with back of a spoon. Chill. Unmold onto lettuce.

## MACARONI SALAD
### (6–8 servings)

1 pound small elbow or bow macaroni
1 cup chopped celery
½ cup chopped sweet onion
1 small green pepper, chopped
1 cup Boiled Dressing*
¼ teaspoon oregano
1–2 teaspoons minced parsley
Lettuce
2 tomatoes (optional)

Cook the macaroni following package instructions. Drain and chill. Mix with the celery, onion, and pepper. Toss with the dressing and with oregano and parsley. Serve on lettuce with peeled tomato wedges or slices if you wish.

## RICE SALAD
### (4–6 servings)

2 cups cooked rice
3 tomatoes, peeled and sliced
2 green peppers, cut into strips
½ teaspoon salt
¼ teaspoon pepper
2 tablespoons oil
1 tablespoon vinegar
1 teaspoon prepared mustard
Minced parsley (garnish)

Put the rice, tomatoes, and green pepper in a bowl. Mix the salt and pepper with oil, vinegar, and mustard. Pour into the salad and stir gently. Sprinkle with a little parsley if you wish.

# Molded Salads

Aspics are the jewels of the salad family. They go well by themselves, or served first, filled with something light, or eaten last, molded or filled with fruit, or providing the main course at luncheon or supper, surrounding something substantial. A tomato aspic typically comes first, a fruit concoction last.

An aspic is a set piece, interesting in its form as well as in its glowing color. You deliberately select the mold that will do the most for the dish, deep enough to bring out the inner gleam of the aspic, and perhaps faceted to make it sparkle like a gemstone; or you can use any bowl to produce a cabochon jewel; or small molds out of custard cups can march around the filling in a circle. Mousses don't glow; they are opaque but are equally decorative and delicious.

An unusual aspic can bring variety to the meat course. Tired of cranberry sauce? Why not try Cranberry Mold with your turkey? Why not serve Prune Aspic with duck, Asparagus Mousse with ham, and Cucumber Aspic with fish?

All molded salads add glamor to a meal. They are a little trouble but it is time spent ahead. They must be made several hours before they are served. If you make this kind of a salad, you will be free at the last minute.

To unmold an aspic or mousse run the tip of a small knife around the edge of the bowl, invert over a platter—if the salad doesn't pop out, try to pry it gently with a fork or put a warm cloth over the bottom of the mold for a few moments, or dip the mold in hot water.

### BASIC TOMATO ASPIC
(*6–8 servings*)

3½ tablespoons gelatin
3 cups tomato juice
1 cup consommé
¼ cup sugar
½ teaspoon salt
2–3 tablespoons vinegar

Sprinkle the gelatin on 1 cup of the cold tomato juice. Heat the remaining 2 cups of tomato juice with the consommé, sugar, salt, and vinegar, and pour onto the gelatin. Stir to dissolve. Pour into a large mold or 6 to 8 individual cups. Chill until set.

### HERBED TOMATO ASPIC
(*8 servings*)

¼ cup chopped celery
⅛ cup chopped onion
1 teaspoon salt
⅛ teaspoon freshly ground pepper
1 tablespoon sugar
½ teaspoon basil
1 tablespoon vinegar
1 bay leaf, crushed
2 cups tomato juice
2 tablespoons gelatin
1 cup Mayonnaise*

Cook the celery and onion with the seasonings in tomato juice until they are very soft. Strain. Mix the gelatin in ½ cup cold water, and add to the hot tomato mixture. Stir to dissolve. Pour into a ring mold if you're filling it with seafood or other salad. Serve with Mayonnaise.

## TOMATO ASPIC
### (8 servings)

3 cups tomato juice
½ teaspoon celery salt
1 tablespoon prepared mustard
½ teaspoon onion salt
½ teaspoon salt
⅛ teaspoon pepper
2 envelopes unflavored gelatin
Salad greens
1 cup Mayonnaise* or Herb Mayonnaise*

Heat the tomato juice in a pot with celery salt, mustard, onion salt, salt, and pepper. Simmer 3–4 minutes. Add the gelatin (it has been softened in 1 cup cold water). Stir to dissolve and remove from heat. Pour into a wet ring mold. Chill. Serve on crisp greens. You may fill the center with seafood, artichoke hearts, mixed vegetable salad, or almost anything. Serve with Mayonnaise or Herb Mayonnaise.

## VEGETABLES IN ASPIC
### (6 servings)

1 envelope gelatin
1 chicken bouillon cube or ¾ cup broth
½ cup tomato juice
12 cooked asparagus tips
1 cup cooked peas
Lettuce
¾ cup Mayonnaise* or French Dressing*

Soften the gelatin in ¼ cup cold water. Heat the bouillon cube in ¾ cup water and pour over the gelatin to dissolve. Add tomato juice. Pour into a mold to depth of ¼" only. When set, arrange the asparagus tips. Chill. Chill remaining gelatin until syrupy, fold in the peas and add to mold. Chill. Serve on lettuce with Mayonnaise or French Dressing.

### VEGETABLE ASPIC
#### (4 servings)

1 envelope gelatin
1 cup hot chicken or beef broth
1 tablespoon lemon juice
½ teaspoon salt
¼ teaspoon pepper
1 cup mixed chopped vegetables, carrots, cucumbers, celery
1 tablespoon minced scallions
1 teaspoon minced parsley

Soften the gelatin in ¼ cup cold water and add ¼ cup hot broth; stir to dissolve. Add remaining broth, lemon juice, salt, and pepper. Chill until the mixture begins to get thick. Mix in the vegetables, scallions, and parsley. Pour into a mold and chill.

### CUCUMBER ASPIC
#### (4 servings)

1 package lemon gelatin
1 envelope unflavored gelatin
¼ teaspoon salt
2 cucumbers, peeled
1 tablespoon lemon juice
1 teaspoon chopped onion
¾ cup Mayonnaise*

Mix the lemon gelatin and the unflavored gelatin with salt and 1 cup boiling water. Stir to dissolve the gelatin. Put the cut-up cucumber in a blender with lemon juice and onion. Buzz until mushy and add to the gelatin. Pour into a mold and chill until firm. Serve with Mayonnaise. Especially good with fish.

## HAM ASPIC
### (6 *servings*)

1 envelope gelatin
1½ pounds cooked ham, ground
1 teaspoon lemon juice
1 cup minced celery
1 onion, grated
1 cup tomato juice
Lettuce

Soften the gelatin in ½ cup hot water and pour over the ham.
Add remaining ingredients and pour into a mold. Chill until set.
Unmold onto shredded lettuce.

## PRUNE ASPIC
### (8 *servings*)

2 envelopes gelatin
2 cups prune juice
2 cups pitted coarsely chopped cooked prunes
2 tablespoons lemon juice
1 teaspoon grated lemon rind

Dissolve the gelatin in ½ cup water, and stir in the heated prune
juice to dissolve the gelatin. Let thicken slightly, then stir in the
prunes, lemon juice, and rind. Pour into a mold and chill.

Especially good with meat such as veal, ham, or roast pork.

## TONGUE IN ASPIC
### (6 *servings*)

1 envelope gelatin
2 (10½ ounce) cans beef bouillon
Salt and pepper
1½ pounds cooked smoked tongue, sliced very thin
1 (1 pound) can tiny peas
Water cress and/or greens

Soften the gelatin in ⅓ cup hot water. Add the bouillon and season to taste with a little salt and pepper. Coat the bottom of a ring mold with aspic and chill. Dip the tongue slices into the remaining aspic and line the mold with overlapping slices and chill again. Add the peas and pour in remaining aspic. Chill until set. Unmold on round platter and fill center and garnish sides with water cress. If water cress is not available, use other greens.

## ASPARAGUS MOUSSE
### (6–8 *servings*)

1 envelope gelatin
1 tablespoon vinegar
1 tablespoon lemon juice
1 teaspoon salt
⅛ teaspoon pepper
Dash paprika
3 cups cooked, diced asparagus
1 tablespoon minced pimento
1 teaspoon minced onion

Dissolve gelatin in a little cold water. Reserve 1 cup of water asparagus was cooked in. Boil down to about ½ cup and add hot. Stir to dissolve. Add all seasonings and chill until syrupy. Fold in the asparagus, pimento, and onions. Pour into a mold and chill.

## SALMON MOUSSE
### (6 *servings*)

1 envelope gelatin
¼ cup vinegar
1 teaspoon dry mustard
½ teaspoon salt
1 small onion, chopped
1 (1 pound) can salmon
½ cup chopped celery
Few sprigs parsley
½ cup heavy cream, whipped

Soften the gelatin in ½ cup hot water and put in blender with
vinegar, mustard, salt, and onion. Blend for a minute, then add
the salmon, juice and all, and the celery and parsley. Blend until
smooth—about a minute. Combine with the whipped cream and
pour into a mold and chill.

## TUNA MOUSSE

Make exactly as you do the Salmon Mousse, substituting tuna
for the salmon.

## ROQUEFORT MOUSSE
### (6 *servings*)

1 envelope gelatin
1 teaspoon salt
¼ teaspoon pepper
¼ pound Roquefort or blue cheese
2 tablespoons minced scallions or chives
½ cup minced celery
1 cup heavy cream, whipped
Salad greens
1 cup French Dressing*

Soften gelatin in ¼ cup cold water. Add 1 cup boiling water and stir to dissolve. Add salt and pepper and chill until syrupy. Mash the cheese and mix with scallions or chives, and celery. Fold the cheese mixture into whipped cream and add to the gelatin. Pour into a wet ring, or other mold, and chill. Serve on salad greens with French Dressing.

### LIGHT LEMON ROQUEFORT MOLD
#### (6 *servings*)

1 package lemon gelatin
2 tablespoons vinegar
3 ounces Roquefort cheese
3 ounces cream cheese
½ cup heavy cream, whipped

Dissolve the gelatin in ¾ cup of boiling water. Add the vinegar. Mix the cheeses together until smooth, and add to the gelatin. Fold in the whipped cream, and turn into a wet ring mold or other mold. Chill.

### CRANBERRY MOLD
#### (6 *servings*)

2 envelopes gelatin
¾ cup sugar
1 tablespoon lemon juice
Juice 1 orange
1 cup raw ground cranberries
Ground rind 1 orange
1 tablespoon grated lemon rind
½ cup crushed pineapple
1 cup chopped celery

Dissolve the gelatin in ½ cup water. Add hot juice from the pineapple, and stir to dissolve. Add sugar, lemon and orange juices. Chill until thickened. Stir in the remaining ingredients, and pour into a ring or other mold.

Good with turkey or chicken.

## PINEAPPLE CHEESE MOUSSE
### (6 *servings*)

- 2 envelopes unflavored gelatin
- 1 can crushed pineapple
- 3 tablespoons lemon juice
- ⅓ cup sugar
- Pinch salt
- ⅓ pound Cheddar cheese, shredded
- 1 cup heavy cream, whipped

Soften the gelatin in ½ cup cold water. Add the heated pineapple and stir to dissolve the gelatin. Remove at once from heat. Add lemon juice, sugar and salt. Chill until syrupy. Fold in the cheese and cream. Pour into a mold and chill until firm.

## GRAPEFRUIT AVOCADO MOLD
### (6 *servings*)

- 1 package lime gelatin
- 1 envelope unflavored gelatin
- ½ cup grapefruit juice
- 2 grapefruit
- 1 large avocado
- 1 teaspoon lime or lemon juice
- ½ cup chopped celery

Soften the gelatin in ¼ cup cold water, add 2 cups boiling water and stir to dissolve. Add the grapefruit juice. Chill until syrupy. Peel and section the grapefruit. Peel and slice the avocado and sprinkle with a little lime or lemon juice. Mix the grapefruit, avocado and celery into the gelatin. Pour into a mold and chill. Unmold on a platter to serve.

# Fruit Salads

Fruit salads, chilled or frozen, take their place beside the aspics and mousses. An infinite variety of fruit salads, all delicious, may be presented in a wide choice of ways. Take a pineapple, for instance, split it lengthwise, plumes and all, and scoop out the meat. Now freeze the shell. After a couple of hours, it comes out of your freezer like a solid ceramic bowl realistically modeled in the fruit shape. Frozen hard, it will not drip nor wilt, and besides it keeps the contents well chilled. The contents will be the pineapple bits, sugared and chilled and combined with any suitable fruit, best of all strawberries; use a fruit French Dressing. For a children's party, make an orange basket by cutting a large orange in half and scooping out the fruit, pulp, and core. Scallop the edge with a scissors or sharp knife. Fill the shell with citrus or mixed fruit salad or sugared grapes. You can freeze the shells for a colder salad.

### SUNBURST SALAD
#### (6 servings)

2 cups grapefruit sections
2 cups orange sections
Lettuce
1 (3 ounce) package cream cheese
2 tablespoons heavy cream
¼ cup French Dressing* or Lemon French Dressing*

For each serving arrange the fruit sections, petal fashion, on lettuce. In the center place cream cheese slightly softened with cream and whipped until fluffy. Serve with French Dressing or Lemon French Dressing.

## ORANGE AND WATER CRESS SALAD
### (6 *servings*)

4 oranges
1 stalk celery
¼ teaspoon sugar
¼ cup Lemon French Dressing*
1 bunch water cress

Section the oranges and shred the celery. Add sugar to the Lemon French Dressing. Pour it over a mixture of the orange and celery. Pile this on water cress which has been put into a salad bowl.

## ORANGE AND CELERY SALAD
### (6 *servings*)

6 oranges
¾ cup chopped celery
¼ cup Fruit French Dressing*
Salad greens
Chopped mint (optional)

Section the oranges and combine with celery, and dressing, and let stand a few hours to marinate. Serve on crisp greens, and sprinkle with mint if you wish.

## ORANGE ONION SALAD
### (6 *servings*)

6 oranges
1 large sweet onion, sliced thin
½ cup French Dressing*
Few strips of pimento
Greens

Peel and slice the oranges and combine with the onion. Marinate for about an hour in the French Dressing. Garnish with pimento and serve on crisp salad greens.

## ORANGE AND OLIVE SALAD
### (4 servings)

4 blood oranges, peeled and sliced thin
2 sweet onions, sliced thin
½ pound black olives
2 tablespoons olive oil
Pinch salt
½ teaspoon sugar

Mix the oranges and onions. Add the pitted olives, cut in half. Pour the oil, to which you have added a pinch of salt and sugar, over the salad.

## GRAPEFRUIT AND AVOCADO SALAD
### (4 servings)

2 avocados
2 tablespoons lemon juice
2 grapefruit, sectioned
1 bunch water cress
1 (3 ounce) package cream cheese (optional)
½ cup Lemon French Dressing*

Cut the avocados in half lengthwise, peel, and slice. Dip in lemon juice to prevent darkening. Place alternate sections of grapefruit and sliced avocado, petal fashion, on the water cress. Roll the cream cheese into balls, and place balls around the salad if you wish. Serve with Lemon French Dressing.

## GRAPEFRUIT, PERSIMMON, AND AVOCADO SALAD
### (8 servings)

2 avocados
1–2 tablespoons lemon juice
French Dressing* or Lemon French Dressing*
2 grapefruit
2 persimmons
Boston or Bibb lettuce

Peel and cut the avocados into thick slices and sprinkle with a little lemon juice. Section the grapefruit, being careful to avoid the membrane. Cut the persimmons into eighths. Arrange the soft lettuce on a plate and alternate pieces of avocado, grapefruit, and the persimmons. Top with the dressing mixed with a tablespoon or two of juice from the grapefruit.

## CHERRY SALAD
### (6 *servings*)

½ pint small curd cottage cheese
1–2 tablespoons cream
⅛ teaspoon salt
1 pound fresh large black Bing cherries
Lettuce
1 cup Fruit French Dressing*

Soften the cheese with cream and add the salt. Remove the pits from the cherries and fill with the cheese, letting some cheese stick out from the opening of the cherries. Arrange the filled cherries on lettuce and pass the Fruit French Dressing.

## CHERRIES AND CREAM CHEESE
### (4–6 *servings*)

1 (3 ounce) package cream cheese
3 tablespoons heavy cream
1 pound fresh cherries or 1 large can Bing cherries, pitted
Salad greens
½ cup Mayonnaise*

Soften the cheese with 1 tablespoon cream, and fill the cherries with this mixture. Serve on salad greens. Thin the Mayonnaise with the remaining cream, and serve with the salad.

## SPICY PEACH OR PEAR SALAD
### (6 servings)

⅓ cup vinegar
1 stick cinnamon
⅓ cup sugar
6 whole cloves
6 halves of cooked or canned peaches or pears
½ cup cream cheese or cottage cheese
3 tablespoons Mayonnaise*

Add ¼ cup water to the vinegar in a sauce pan. Put in the cinnamon, sugar, and cloves, and simmer 5 minutes. Pour over the fruit and chill. Drain and put the fruit hollow side up on lettuce. Fill centers with cream cheese or cottage cheese mixed with the Mayonnaise.

## PEACH AND CHEESE SALAD
### (4–8 servings)

1 (¼ pound) package small curd cottage cheese
1 tablespoon cream
8 canned peach halves
Lettuce
Paprika
¼ cup chopped nuts (optional)
1–1½ cups Boiled Dressing* or Sour Cream Dressing*

Soften the cheese with cream and a tablespoon or two of juice from the peaches. Fill the peach halves with this. Place on lettuce cups or shredded lettuce and sprinkle with a little paprika and chopped nuts, if you wish. Pass Boiled Dressing or Sour Cream Dressing.

## PEAR AND CHEESE SALAD

Make exactly like the Peach and Cheese Salad, substituting canned or fresh pears for the peaches.

## WALDORF SALAD
### (4 servings)

    2 cups diced apples
    1 cup diced celery
    ½ cup Mayonnaise*
    Broken or coarsely chopped walnuts
    Lettuce

Mix the apple, celery, and Mayonnaise. Toss until both are well coated with Mayonnaise. Serve in a chilled bowl, top with walnuts, and put a border of lettuce around.

## PEAR WALDORF SALAD

Substitute cut up fresh pears for the apples in Waldorf Salad.

## APPLE AND CELERY SALAD
### (6 servings)

    ½ cup diced apple
    ½ cup diced celery
    ¼ cup Mayonnaise*
    1 head lettuce
    6 slices bacon

Mix the apple, celery, and Mayonnaise. Break the lettuce into bite-size pieces. If using firm lettuce such as iceberg, shred it. Cook the bacon and dice it or cut into thin strips. Toss all together or put half the lettuce in a bowl, add bacon to remaining lettuce, and toss with the apple and celery.

## CRANBERRY ORANGE SALAD
### (6–8 *servings*)

1 pound raw cranberries
2 small oranges
1 cup sugar
Lettuce (optional)
10 small marshmallows (optional)

Put the cranberries and cut up oranges, peel and all, through a meat grinder. Stir in the sugar. Serve on lettuce. If you wish, cut up the marshmallows with wet scissors and add to the salad.

## CRANBERRY-ORANGE MOLD
### (8 *servings*)

2 cups cranberry juice cocktail
2 packages orange flavored gelatin
1 cup orange juice
4 oranges, peeled and sectioned
1 cup coarsely chopped walnuts

Heat cranberry juice and pour over the gelatin, which has been softened with ¼ cup water. Chill until syrupy, about 45 minutes. Pour half the gelatin into a mold. Let refrigerate 30 minutes. Add orange juice and sections, walnuts and remaining gelatin. Chill until firm. To unmold, run a knife around the edge, invert over a plate, and hold a hot cloth over the mold for a few moments. A good dessert aspic.

## GRAPE ALMOND SALAD
### (6 *servings*)

Soft lettuce, preferably bronze or other garden lettuce
2 cups seedless or seeded grapes
¾ cup toasted almonds
½ cup Lemon French Dressing*
¼ teaspoon ground coriander or curry

Break up the lettuce into a dessert or salad bowl. Cover with grapes and sprinkle with almonds. Pour the dressing mixed with coriander or curry over the salad and toss at table.

### PLUM SALAD
(*6 servings*)

3 pounds fresh plums
Lettuce, shredded
½ cup Mayonnaise*
1 tablespoon minced fresh tarragon or 1 teaspoon dried
1 tablespoon sugar
1 tablespoon tarragon vinegar
½ cup heavy cream, whipped

Cut the plums in slices or wedges. Arrange on individual plates or in a salad bowl, on shredded lettuce. Mix the Mayonnaise with tarragon, sugar, tarragon vinegar, and whipped cream. Pour over the plums. You may make this with canned plums draining off most of the liquid.

# Dessert Salads

Here is summertime magnificence. Melon makes a magnificent salad served first or for a meal ending. Chunks, slices, cubes, or balls of melon may be served alone, with other fruits, or combined with each other. Spanish melon, cantaloupe, Persian, honeydew, casaba, or cranshaw if used in combinations should be chosen for contrasting color flesh. Melon should be served cold and may be marinated in wine, French dressing, or sprinkled with a little rum or sherry. Fruits, hot or cold, with or without a liqueur or wine, are delicious desserts.

### HONEYDEW RING FRUIT SALAD
#### (6 servings)

1 large honeydew melon, peeled
Lettuce
2 cups cantaloupe balls
2 cups fresh raspberries (optional)
2 cups seedless grapes
Sprigs of mint
¾ cup French Dressing*

Slice the melon into 6 thick rings, removing seeds. Put rings on lettuce, and fill the centers with cantaloupe balls, raspberries if available, and grapes. Garnish with mint. Serve with French Dressing.

## DOUBLE MELON SALAD
### (4 servings)

1 cantaloupe, peeled
Leaf lettuce
2 cups watermelon balls
1½ cups honeydew melon balls
Sprigs of mint (garnish)
¾ cup Sherry Mayonnaise*

Slice the cantaloupe into rings about an inch thick and remove seeds. Place on lettuce on salad plates. Fill each ring with watermelon and honeydew balls. Garnish with sprigs of mint, if you wish. Serve with Sherry Mayonnaise.

## WATERMELON BOWL SALAD
### (6 servings)

Designed to impress people at your next patio party, this watermelon half is filled with chilled melon balls, pineapple slices, and blueberries. It's also distinctive as a buffet centerpiece. Remember, choose a handsome melon.

½ watermelon
2 cups cantaloupe balls
2 cups pineapple chunks
1 cup blueberries
Greens
1 cup Lemon French Dressing*
2 tablespoons honey (optional)

With a ball cutter, remove the center from half of a short thick watermelon. Scrape out remaining flesh, and put shell in deep freezer. Toss together the watermelon and cantaloupe balls, pineapple chunks, and blueberries. Chill. Place the watermelon bowl on greens on a platter, and fill it with the mixed fruit. Serve with Lemon French Dressing, add honey to the dressing, if you wish.

## APRICOTS WITH LIQUEUR
### (4 servings)

12 very ripe fresh apricots
3 ounces Grand Marnier, Cointreau or Curaçao

Plunge the apricots into boiling water for a moment and they will peel easily. Slice them into a bowl and pour over the liqueur of your choice. This salad may be made with drained canned apricots.

## FRUIT AS FINGER FOOD

Cut fruit, such as pineapple, apple, pear, or melon, into sticks, thick or thin, or cut into wedges. Arrange assortment on a platter and pass sauce for dunking the fruit.

## FRUIT PLATTER
### (8 servings)

1 melon
2 apples or pears
4 peaches or apricots
4 slices pineapple
2 bananas
1½ cups Fruit French Dressing*

Choose a ripe cantaloupe or small honeydew. Peel and cut into spears or wedges. Core and cut the apples or pears into eighths, the peaches or apricots into quarters, the pineapple into wedges, and the bananas into slices. The banana will discolor, so add it last. Serve the dressing in little bowls or sauce dishes so that each can dunk his fruit into the dressing.

## CALIFORNIA FRUIT SALAD
### (6–8 *servings*)

2 grapefruit, sectioned
4 oranges, sectioned
3 peaches fresh or canned, cut up
1 cup seedless or seeded grapes
1 cup cut up pineapple
1 cup diced melon
½ cup Fruit Mayonnaise*
2 tablespoons orange juice
1 teaspoon lemon juice
½ cup sweetened whipped cream

Mix the fruits together in a chilled bowl, preferably glass. Mix the Mayonnaise with orange juice, lemon juice, and the whipped cream, and serve with the salad or toss into the salad.

## WHITE WINE FRUIT MOLD
### (6 *servings*)

2 packages lemon gelatin
¾ cup white wine (sauterne type)
2–2½ cups cut up mixed fruit (peaches, pears, apricots, plums, bananas, seedless grapes, and/or cherries)
1 teaspoon lemon juice
½ cup nuts (walnuts, pecans, or almonds) (optional)

Soften the gelatin in 1¼ cup boiling water. Add wine and cool. Add fruit, lemon juice, and nuts if you wish. Pour into a mold and chill. If you use canned fruits, be sure to drain and use ½ cup juice in place of ½ cup of the water. Use a mixture of the suggested fruits.

## PORT APPLESAUCE MOLD
### (6 servings)

1 envelope unflavored gelatin or 1 package lemon or rasp-
    berry flavored gelatin
½ cup port wine
1 teaspoon lemon juice
1 tablespoon grated orange peel
1 (1 pound 1 ounce) can applesauce
½ cup whipped cream or sour cream (garnish)

Soften the gelatin in ½ cup of water. Add the hot wine and stir
until gelatin is dissolved. Add lemon juice, orange peel, and hot
applesauce. Pour into an oiled mold. Chill until firm. Turn out
on a plate. Good with roast pork or duck. If serving as a dessert,
garnish with slightly sweetened whipped or sour cream.

## HOT PEAR DESSERT
### (6 servings)

6 canned pears
Apple and/or mint jelly
Coarsely chopped candied ginger and/or orange peel
2 tablespoons rum

Lay pear halves on a piece of foil. Fill the centers with jelly and
crystallized ginger or orange peel. Sprinkle with rum and wrap
carefully cut side up in foil. Bake 10–15 minutes in 450° oven.

## BROILED GRAPEFRUIT
### (4 servings)

2 large grapefruit
4 tablespoons rum
4 tablespoons warm honey
Mace

Cut the grapefruit in half, cut out the core and loosen each section from the skin with a sharp pointed knife or grapefruit knife. Do not cut the membrane between the sections, run the knife around each section not around the outside. Mix the rum and honey, and pour over the grapefruit. Sprinkle with a pinch of mace. Broil for 10 minutes to brown top; or wrap in aluminum foil, cut side up, and broil 15–20 minutes. Unwrap to serve.

## PINEAPPLE SLICES FLAMBE
### (4–6 servings)

1 pineapple
¼–½ cup brown sugar
¼ pound butter
¼ cup rum

Cut the pineapple into ½ inch slices and place on a baking sheet. Sprinkle with brown sugar, and dot with butter. Broil until the sugar and butter melt and are light brown. Immediately transfer to a fireproof dish. Pour the heated rum over and ignite.

## FROZEN FRUIT SALAD
### (6 servings)

½ cup cherries, pitted and cut in half
½ cup pears, diced
½ cup peaches, diced
½ cup pineapple, diced
2 tablespoons powdered sugar
½ cup Mayonnaise*
1 teaspoon lemon juice
1 cup heavy cream, whipped
½ cup Mayonnaise* (optional)

Mix the fruits and drain reserving ½ cup of the juice from the fruit. Mix the sugar, Mayonnaise, and lemon juice. Fold in the fruit and whipped cream. Put into a wet mold and freeze. Serve with Mayonnaise if you wish.

## EASY FROZEN FRUIT SALAD
### (8 *servings*)

1 envelope gelatin
2 tablespoons lemon juice
½ cup Mayonnaise*
1 (1 pound 13 ounce) can fruit cocktail
1 cup heavy cream, whipped

Soften the gelatin in ¼ cup hot water. Combine with lemon juice, Mayonnaise, and ¼ cup juice from the fruit. Pour in the drained fruit and fold in the cream. Freeze until almost firm. The fruit should not be frozen too hard.

## FROZEN PINEAPPLE SALAD
### (8 *servings*)

1½ cups crushed drained pineapple
¼ cup maraschino cherries
6 marshmallows, cut up
2 tablespoons sugar
1 (8 ounce) package cream cheese
3 tablespoons Mayonnaise*
1 cup heavy cream, whipped
Lettuce (optional)

Mix the pineapple, cherries, and marshmallows, and add sugar. Soften the cheese with the Mayonnaise. When smooth, fold in the whipped cream. Add the fruit. Pour into a mold, bowl, or refrigerator tray, and freeze until firm. Serve on lettuce, if you wish.

# Chapter Three

## SALAD DAYS AROUND THE GLOBE

"*Et ensuite, de la salade, madame, naturellement,*" ruled the *maître d'hôtel* at a Michelin three-star restaurant, creating a menu. "*Mais oui!*" I cried.

"*Und Dazu, Kartoffelsalat, natürlich,*" urged the *Kellner* in the Rathskeller. "*Natürlich!*" I agreed.

"*Borani Esfanaj!*" cried the Iranian waiter in a flood of voluble Persian. Of course I nodded, even if I didn't understand him. I soon found that the spinach salad he suggested, blended with yogurt and garlic, made the perfect complement to the skewered broiled lamb; just as the German potato salad pointed up the *Nierenbraten*, and the French tarragon-flavored greens set off the rich *coq au vin*.

I first encountered foreign salads tagging along with my father on his gastronomic tours of Europe, trundling from repast to repast in the high Peugeot touring car. Often the repast was a luncheon alfresco by the roadside. Majestic in his voluminous dun-colored duster, his high silk hat laid aside in favor of a hound's-tooth-check motoring cap, Father would descend from the high step, hand down my mother, and direct operations. The chauffeur spread the white damask cloth, my mother unpacked the replete hamper, and my sister and I watched impatiently. Out of the hampers would come wine and wineglasses, a long crusty French loaf, a fat sausage, native cheese, and some madeleines.

Because Father thought no meal was complete without its green course, there might be radishes and sweet butter, or fennel, or sometimes a white asparagus. It was best of all when Father spied lamb's-tongues or dandelion in the field or water cress in the stream. Then an expedition was organized, with Father in command and Carol and my sister Rhoda as skirmishers. We liked the water cress best because it gave us an excuse to get wet; and good eating it was too, crisp and pungent from the cold, tumbling water, with no dressing at all.

Even when we didn't pick it fresh for him, Father never failed to call for salad whenever he lunched or dined. Still under his influence decades later, I keep on trotting around the world, sampling the best salad specialties of every country I visit, East or West. On foreign tables, I have found, salads are seldom the star performer; but each country has its own typical favorites. The variety is great, from green Chinese salad to the green and red of Sweet Pepper Salad to White Hearts of Palm Salad to Greek *Taramasalata*, a blending of pink roe, to pepper-red Mexican *Ceviche*, made with raw fish and—it sometimes seems—GUN-POWDER.

Every foreign menu is a new adventure, and sometimes a heroic one.

In Hong Kong as I prepared to dine out with Maple Quong, the Hurok of Hong Kong, I was glad to think about dining out Chinese style. Chinese style, as I understood it, decrees that the soup ends the meal.

Twelve of us sat down to the table, with a silent servitor in white standing behind every chair. As course followed course, they were ready to furnish fresh plates and hot towels. One new sensation succeeded another: the chicken breasts with black mushrooms were sensational, the minced quail was even better, the pork with crisp Chinese vegetables and fresh water chestnuts was as good as a salad. After I had done honor to six such dishes centering the table in turn, I was glad to see the bowl of soup appear.

It was shark fin soup, and the best soup I ever tasted. My host seeing how fast my bowlful was disappearing, courteously ladled me a refill. I had just a small cranny left to stow it in. Knowing this was the end, I stowed it.

Imagine my surprise, when vinegared vegetables appeared "to clear our palates," and the whole thing started over!

What did this mean?

"It is the custom," explained my dinner partner, "to salute the honored guest at a formal dinner, by counting one course for each guest, and one over."

Of course the honored guest had to pay tribute to every one of the thirteen courses by eating it. I was never more convinced that "a little learning is a dangerous thing."

Thus I arrived in Bangkok pretty wary of Oriental feasting.

"Madam's plane was late," fretted the desk clerk. "You must make haste to be ready. The car will call in five minutes to take you to a luncheon with the Princess Chumbhot."

"I can't possibly make it!"

The clerk's mouth and eyes opened wide.

"You will be ready," he said with finality. "You will not keep the princess waiting."

I was ready.

I wouldn't have missed it. The princess welcomed me to a classic Siamese house soaring on stilts, and sat me down to a classic Siamese meal which did *not* conclude with soup. I enjoyed every bite.

"And tomorrow night," proposed the princess, "I will take you and your escort to a formal dinner at my cousin's, Prince Pandit, in honor of Marlon Brando and the cast of *The Ugly American!*"

"A formal dinner!" I said wistfully. "How can you wedge in two crashers at a formal sit-down dinner?"

"Easily," said the princess, "since I am lending my cousin twenty-five of my best servants and all of my tablecloths."

I went. There were 270 guests seated. As I added 270 + 2 and figured out 272 courses, I was glad this was Thailand and not China.

# French Salads

In France, everybody likes to serve salad before or after the main course, because the salad vinegar interferes with the important wines of the meal. French salads go well on the *hors d'oeuvre* plate, or at the end of the main course, accompanied or followed by cheese.

## FRENCH GREEN SALAD
### (*4–6 servings*)

2 heads Boston or other soft lettuce
¼ cup French Dressing*

Wash the lettuce and pull the leaves apart. Spread out to dry thoroughly. Break up only the larger outside leaves. Put into a salad bowl. Add the dressing and toss gently.

## FRENCH MIXED GREEN SALAD
### (*6 servings*)

1 head romaine
1 head Boston lettuce
1 chapon—being a crust of French bread with a clove of garlic inserted into it
½ teaspoon salt
¼ teaspoon freshly ground pepper
⅓ cup French Dressing*
3 hard boiled egg yolks

Wash, dry, and tear up the greens. Rub bowl with the chapon and leave it in the bowl. Add the greens and salt and pepper. Just before serving, add the French Dressing and toss. Sprinkle with grated hard cooked egg yolks.

## FRENCH WATER CRESS SALAD
### (4 servings)

1 bunch water cress
½ teaspoon salt
Freshly ground pepper
3 tablespoons olive oil
1 tablespoon lemon juice or wine vinegar (optional)

Wash the water cress thoroughly in several changes of water. Dry and refrigerate. When ready to serve, cut off tough stem ends and toss with salt, pepper, and oil. You may add lemon juice or vinegar if you wish. If serving good wine, omit the lemon or vinegar.

## PARISIAN SALAD
### (4–6 servings)

1–1½ cups strips of cooked beef or veal
1 cup sliced cooked potatoes
1 onion, parboiled and sliced thin
2 tomatoes, peeled and sliced
Soft lettuce
½ cup French Dressing*
1 tablespoon minced parsley

Mix the beef with potatoes, onion, and tomatoes. Put onto lettuce leaves and break a few leaves into small pieces and add to the salad. Pour the dressing over and sprinkle with parsley. Toss at the table.

## FRENCH BEAN AND TOMATO SALAD
### SALADE DE HARICOTS VERTS ET TOMATES
(6 *servings*)

1 pound French cut beans or 2 boxes frozen
1 teaspoon salt
2 large tomatoes
½ cup French Dressing*

Cook the beans in salted water until just tender. Rinse at once in cold water. Drain and chill. If using frozen beans, cook according to instructions. Put the beans in a bowl with the peeled, quartered tomatoes and pour the French Dressing over. Toss gently.

## FRENCH TOMATO SALAD
(6 *servings*)

6 tomatoes
4 tablespoons oil
1 tablespoon vinegar
1 teaspoon salt
Freshly ground pepper
½ teaspoon sugar
2 tablespoons minced parsley
2 shallots, minced

Peel the tomatoes and slice thin. Place the tomatoes on a cold platter so they overlap a little. Mix the remaining ingredients thoroughly. Pour the dressing over.

# Italian Salads

The Italian salad, like the Italian genius, is spicy, original, and varied. Tossed salads are piquant with fresh herbs flavoring fragrant greens and raw mushrooms. For an *antipasto*, raw vegetables which have been soaked with garlic in salted ice water are dipped by each diner in seasoned olive oil. Celery, fennel, radishes, baby artichokes, strips of green pepper, and tiny carrots emerge fresh and crunchy from their garlic-flavored bath.

## ITALIAN SALAD BOWL
### (6 *servings*)

2 heads soft lettuce
1 small iceberg lettuce
½ bunch curly endive
1 cup julienne strips salami
¼ cup French Dressing*
Pinch oregano
1 clove garlic, crushed

Tear the greens into bite-size pieces, and put into a salad bowl with the salami. Toss lightly with the French Dressing, oregano, and garlic.

## ITALIAN TOMATO SALAD
### (6 *servings*)

6 large tomatoes
1 tablespoon oregano, or 1 teaspoon dried
½ teaspoon salt
¼ teaspoon pepper
2 tablespoons olive oil

Peel and slice the tomatoes and arrange on a platter. Sprinkle with oregano, salt and pepper. Dribble the oil over and let stand a number of hours.

## ITALIAN SEAFOOD SALAD
### *INSALATA DI FRUTTI DI MARE*
### (6 *servings*)

1 cup cleaned small clams
1 cup lobster meat
1 cup crabmeat
1 cup small shrimp
1 cup mussels (if available)
½ cup white wine
1 cup cut up squid (optional)
1 cup diced celery

Clams, lobster meat, crab, and shrimp; these are probably all available at your fish market. If you use mussels, steam 2 pounds with 2 pounds of clams in ½ cup of water and white wine. Remove from shell and set aside. Let the broth settle and pour off the top being careful to avoid sand. Cook the cut up lobster and crab in this broth for 20 minutes. If the shrimp are not cooked, they should also be cooked in the broth, but take only 5 minutes after the broth comes to a boil. Mix all of the seafood together with the celery. If the shrimp are large, cut them in half. You need about 4 cups of seafood for 6 people as a luncheon or main course dish. There must be a variety of fish to give different flavor and texture.

## SEAFOOD SAUCE

½ cup olive oil
1 teaspoon salt
¼ teaspoon white pepper
¼ teaspoon mustard
¼ teaspoon paprika
⅛ cup wine vinegar
Juice 1 lemon
1 tablespoon minced anchovies

Blend all of the ingredients together. Pour over the fish salad and let stand for an hour in the refrigerator.

## SALAD WITH MUSHROOMS
### INSALATA DI OVOLI
(4 servings)

1 cup very thinly sliced mushrooms
⅓ cup julienne carrots
⅓ cup julienne celery
½ cup thinly sliced Swiss cheese
¼ cup oil
⅛ cup vinegar
1 teaspoon salt
¼ teaspoon pepper

Do not wash the mushrooms; if they are sandy, wipe them with a damp cloth and cut them as thin as possible. Cut the carrots into matchstick pieces and the Swiss cheese the same size. Mix the oil, vinegar, salt, and pepper, and pour the mixture over the mushrooms, carrots, celery, and cheese. Toss gently. Chill.

## SICILIAN SALAD
### (4 *servings*)

1 large head lettuce
1 (2¼ ounce) can pitted ripe olives
2 oranges, peeled and sliced thin
¼ cup oil
¼ cup orange juice
1 tablespoon lemon or lime juice
1 teaspoon salt
¼ teaspoon paprika

Break the lettuce into bite-size pieces. Put into a deep platter or shallow salad bowl. Scatter olives and oranges over the greens. Make a dressing with remaining ingredients and pour over the salad.

## SALAD OF RAW MUSHROOMS
### *INSALATA DI FUNGI CRUDI*
### (4–6 *servings*)

¾ pound mushrooms
½ cup olive oil
Juice 1 large lemon
½ teaspoon salt
¼ teaspoon white pepper
Soft salad greens

Slice the heads of the mushrooms very thin. Mix the oil, lemon juice, salt, and pepper, and pour over the mushrooms. Toss gently and let stand ½ hour. Serve on greens. Wild mushrooms are particularly good served this way.

## ITALIAN BROCCOLI SALAD VINAIGRETTE
### (4 *servings*)

1 bunch broccoli
1 teaspoon salt
1 cup Vinaigrette*
Lettuce or water cress
2 hard boiled eggs (optional)

Trim the ends of the broccoli and peel the stems if they are tough.
Cook in about an inch of salted water until barely tender, about
10–12 minutes. Drain and pour the dressing over while the broccoli is hot. Chill and serve on lettuce or water cress. Garnish
with egg slices or wedges if you wish.

# Swiss Salads

Crossing the Alps into Switzerland, the vertical country of goat-herds, yodeling, and goats cropping edelweiss, salad gains a new dimension. One would expect the Swiss to use Swiss cheese in salad; and so they do.

### SWISS SALAD
(6–8 *servings*)

½ pound Swiss cheese
1 head lettuce
½ pound spinach, or chicory, or 1 bunch water cress
¼ cup Mayonnaise*
1 tablespoon prepared mustard
½ teaspoon paprika
2 tablespoons oil
1 tablespoon wine vinegar

Cut the cheese in julienne strips. Break the greens into bite-size pieces and mix with the cheese. Blend the Mayonnaise with mustard, paprika, oil, and vinegar. Pour over the salad and toss.

### SWISS CHEESE AND ANCHOVY SALAD
(6 *servings*)

1 head soft lettuce
1 cup Swiss cheese, cut in sticks
1 (3 ounce) can anchovy fillets
1 bunch water cress (optional)
¼ cup French Dressing*

Break lettuce into small pieces. Put in bowl and top with cheese and anchovies. Place water cress around the salad if you wish. Pour on the French Dressing and toss at table.

## SWISS LETTUCE AND LEEK SALAD
### (4 servings)

1 head lettuce
3 leeks
3 slices bacon
2–3 tablespoons vinegar
¼ teaspoon salt

Shred the lettuce, and chop the leeks. Mix together. Fry the bacon and crumble it over the salad. Add vinegar and salt to the bacon drippings, and pour warm over the salad.

# German Salads

The Germans, like the Swiss, like their salads solid. Their potato salads are famous. They have a way with cabbage salads. Such salads come to the table on equal terms and at the same time with the good roast meat.

## GERMAN POTATO SALAD WITH SOUR CREAM DRESSING
### KARTOFFELSALAT
### (*4–6 servings*)

2 pounds potatoes, boiled in jackets
¼ cup vinegar
1 tablespoon sugar
1 teaspoon salt
¼ teaspoon pepper
⅛ teaspoon paprika
1 pint sour cream

Peel and slice potatoes while warm. Mix remaining ingredients and pour over potatoes; stir gently.

## GERMAN HOT POTATO SALAD
### (*6 servings*)

2 pounds potatoes, boiled in jackets
6 slices bacon, diced
1 large onion, minced
½ cup vinegar
½ cup beef or chicken broth
1 teaspoon salt
¼ teaspoon pepper
1 teaspoon sugar
2 egg yolks

Peel the potatoes while warm, and slice thin. While the potatoes are cooking, fry the bacon, and when almost crisp add onions. Cook 2 minutes and add the vinegar, broth, and seasonings. Simmer a minute or 2. Remove from heat, and stir into the egg yolks which have been beaten with 2 tablespoons of water. Pour over the potatoes, and mix gently.

## AUSTRIAN POTATO APPLE SALAD
### (6 servings)

3 tablespoons olive oil
3 tablespoons vinegar
½ teaspoon salt
⅛ teaspoon pepper
1 pound potatoes, boiled in jackets
1 pound apples
2 hard boiled eggs
2 cooked beets diced (garnish)

Peel and dice the potatoes. Core, peel, and dice the apples. Make the dressing by mixing oil, vinegar, salt, and pepper. Pour this over a mixture of the potatoes and apples, and garnish with sliced eggs and/or beets.

## AUSTRIAN RED AND WHITE CABBAGE SALAD
### (6 servings)

1 small head white cabbage, shredded
1 small head red cabbage, shredded
2 apples, peeled, cored, and diced
2 tablespoons vinegar
1 teaspoon sugar
½ cup French Dressing*

Mix the red and white cabbage together. Add the apples, vinegar, and sugar, and toss lightly. Then toss in the French Dressing.

## GERMAN COLE SLAW
*(6 servings)*

1 large head cabbage, shredded
1 onion, minced
1 green pepper, diced
2 egg yolks
1 teaspoon salt
¼ teaspoon pepper
⅛ teaspoon dry mustard
1 cup olive oil
3 tablespoons vinegar
1 cup sour cream

Scald the cabbage and squeeze dry. Add the onions and peppers and mix. Put the egg yolks in a bowl with salt and pepper and mustard and add the oil a few drops at a time at first and then in a slow stream beating steadily. Add a little vinegar from time to time. Pour this mixture over the cabbage and then fold in the sour cream.

## GERMAN KNOB CELERY SALAD
*(6 servings)*

2 pounds celery root
2 teaspoons salt
½ cup olive oil
½ cup vinegar
¼ teaspoon pepper
1 tablespoon sugar
1 cup broth
½ teaspoon mustard

Cut the celery into julienne strips and boil in water with 2 teaspoons salt for 5 minutes. Drain and cool. Mix all of the other ingredients. Warm them and pour over the celery root. Chill.

## GERMAN CUCUMBER SALAD
### GURKENSALAT
#### (4 servings)

2 large cucumbers, peeled and sliced thin
2 tablespoons salt
3 tablespoons sour cream
1 tablespoon vinegar or lemon juice
¼ teaspoon sugar
Pinch paprika

Put the cucumbers in a bowl and sprinkle generously with salt. Let stand at least 3 hours. Drain off the water, rinse, and squeeze out any remaining moisture. Put in a bowl and cover with a dressing made by mixing the sour cream, vinegar or lemon juice, and sugar. Sprinkle with paprika.

## GERMAN CHICKEN SALAD
#### (6–8 servings)

½ pound mushrooms, sliced
1–2 tablespoons butter
4–5 cups diced cooked chicken
1½ cups chopped celery
1 cup Mayonnaise*
1 cup heavy cream, whipped
Lettuce
Capers (optional)

Sauté the mushrooms in butter for 2–3 minutes and cool. Mix the chicken, mushrooms, and celery with the Mayonnaise. Let this mixture stand for several hours in the refrigerator. Fold in the cream just before serving. Serve on a bed of lettuce and garnish with capers, if you wish.

# Scandinavian Salads

Herring swims into the salad bowl in Scandinavia. In every guise this favorite fish appears on the smorgasbord table. No spread is complete without a shoal of herring flanked by dilled cucumbers, pickled beets, and lively meat and fish salads.

### HERRING SALAD
### *HERRINGSALAT*
### (6 *servings*)

2 salt herrings
1 dill pickle
1 cucumber
4 apples
6 tablespoons oil
½ cup white wine
¼ cup vinegar
1 onion, minced
⅛ teaspoon salt
⅛ teaspoon pepper
⅛ teaspoon sugar
1 teaspoon dry mustard

Fillet the herring, and dice. Add the pickle and cucumber both diced, and the apples peeled, cored, and diced. Make a dressing out of the oil, white wine, vinegar, and onion. Season with salt, pepper, sugar, and mustard, and pour over the salad.

## NORWEGIAN HERRING SALAD
### (4 servings)

- 1 salt herring
- 1 cup diced pickled beets
- ⅓ cup diced sweet pickles
- ¼ cup chopped onion
- 1 cup diced boiled potatoes
- 2 small apples
- 2 tablespoons sugar
- ¼ cup vinegar
- ¼ cup heavy cream, whipped (optional)

Clean the herring and soak at least overnight in cold water. Skin the fish and cut into dice. Add the beets, pickles, onion, potatoes, and apples, which have been cored, peeled, and diced. Toss gently. Mix the sugar and vinegar with 2 tablespoons cold water, and toss into the salad. Add cream, if you wish.

## SWEDISH MIXED SALAD
### (8 servings)

- 1–2 heads lettuce
- 4 tomatoes
- 2 bunches radishes
- 2 hard boiled eggs
- 1 tablespoon chopped parsley
- 2 tablespoons chopped chives
- ¼ cup French Dressing*

Break the lettuce into bite-size pieces. Peel tomatoes, and slice thin. Slice radishes thin. Chop the egg whites and yolks separately. To assemble the salad, put greens in a salad bowl and arrange slices of tomatoes, radishes, and egg whites, then yolks around the salad. Mix the parsley and chives and put in the center. Just before ready to serve, pour the dressing over and toss salad at the table.

## SWEDISH PICKLED BEET MOLD
### (6 servings)

1 envelope gelatin
Juice ½ lemon
¾ cup sweet pickled beet juice
1 tablespoon horseradish
2 tablespoons vinegar
2 tablespoons grated onion
½ cup diced celery
1 cup chopped pickled beets
½ teaspoon salt
Lettuce
Mayonnaise*

Add 1 cup boiling water to the gelatin and stir to dissolve. Add lemon juice, beet juice, horseradish, vinegar, and onion. Let stand until syrupy, then add the celery and beets, and salt. Turn into a wet or oiled mold. Chill until firm. Turn out on lettuce. Serve with Mayonnaise.

## SWEDISH FROZEN FRUIT SALAD
### FRUKT SALLAD
### (6 servings)

1 (3 ounce) package cream cheese
1 cup heavy cream
2 tablespoons lemon juice
2 tablespoons sugar
⅛ teaspoon salt
1 can fruit cocktail or 2 cups cut up fruit
Lettuce

Soften the cheese with 2 tablespoons of cream. Whip the remaining cream. Add lemon juice, sugar, and salt to the cheese and fold in the whipped cream. Add the drained fruit and stir gently. Freeze in refrigerator tray or mold or shallow bowl. Cut in slices and serve on lettuce. Let stand in refrigerator for half an hour before serving so the fruit won't be too hard.

## DANISH POTATO SALAD
### (6 servings)

4–5 large potatoes, boiled in jackets
4 tablespoons oil
4 tablespoons tarragon vinegar
1 teaspoon salt
1 teaspoon sugar
1 clove garlic, crushed
3 green onions, chopped
6–8 radishes, sliced thin
¼ cup Mayonnaise*
1 tablespoon fresh dill or 1 teaspoon dried
Parsley (garnish)
3 hard cooked eggs (garnish)

Do not overcook the potatoes, peel and cut into ½ inch cubes. Mix oil, vinegar, salt, sugar, and garlic and pour over the potatoes. Chill. When ready to serve, combine the onions and radishes with the potatoes. Mix the Mayonnaise with dill and fold into the salad. Garnish with parsley and hard cooked egg wedges.

## SCANDINAVIAN EGGS STUFFED WITH CUCUMBER
### AGG OCH GURKSALLAD
### (6 servings)

6 hard boiled eggs
1 cup minced cucumber
3 tablespoons Mayonnaise*
¼ teaspoon freshly ground pepper
Few drops onion juice or minced onion (optional)
Parsley sprigs (garnish)
Lettuce

Cut the eggs lengthwise and remove yolks. Drain the cucumber and mix with Mayonnaise and pepper. Add a little onion juice or minced onion, if you wish. Fill the egg whites with the cucumber mixture, and grate egg yolks over the top: garnish with parsley and serve on lettuce.

### SCANDINAVIAN ANCHOVY EGG SALAD
#### (3–4 servings)

8–10 anchovy fillets
1 large onion, minced
2 tablespoons capers
1 egg

Put the chopped anchovies around the edge of a round plate, place a circle of onion inside, next a ring of capers. Put the raw egg in the center, and the person who serves himself first mixes the salad until well blended.

# Spanish and Mexican Salads

Spanish salads like Spanish marriages are arranged with care. Vegetables sprinkled with salt and olive oil are likely to be set out on a flat platter. Graceful, narrow-spouted cruets of oil and vinegar are often ready on the table to bless the happy union.

## GAZPACHO SALAD
### (8 servings)

4 tomatoes, peeled and sliced
2 Italian or 1 Bermuda onion, peeled and sliced thin
2 cucumbers, sliced thin
2 stalks celery, sliced thin
½–¾ cup dry seasoned bread crumbs
½ cup Garlic French Dressing*
Water cress or lettuce (optional)

Place alternate layers of vegetables in a glass bowl. Sprinkle with a few bread crumbs. Chill for at least an hour. Pour the dressing over and toss at table. Serve on water cress or lettuce, if you wish.

## SPANISH ORANGE SALAD
### (6 servings)

½ teaspoon salt
¼ teaspoon freshly ground pepper
¼ teaspoon sugar
¼ cup olive oil
2 tablespoons wine vinegar
3 oranges, peeled and sliced
1 onion
Soft greens
Pimento (garnish)

Mix the salt, pepper, and sugar with oil and vinegar. Pour over the sliced oranges and thinly sliced onion, and let stand for at least one hour. You may peel the oranges or not. Add the greens, which have been broken into small pieces. Garnish with julienne strips of pimento.

### SPANISH OLIVE ANCHOVY SALAD
(*4 servings*)

1 cup pitted olives
4 anchovy fillets
2 tablespoons minced pimento
3 tablespoons olive oil
1 tablespoon wine vinegar
½ teaspoon salt
½ teaspoon mustard
Salad greens

Cut the olives in half. Use green, ripe, or stuffed olives, or a combination. Mince the anchovies and mix with the rest of the ingredients and let stand 2–3 hours. Pour over salad greens, which have been torn into pieces. Toss.

"*Olé!*" cry the hot-blooded Latins south of the border over food that brings tears to American eyes. At a Mexican meal, the cool touch of salad is especially welcome, and fortunately shredded lettuce adorns many a dish.

### MEXICAN EGGPLANT SALAD
(*6 servings*)

1 large eggplant
Juice of 1 lemon
1 tablespoon salt
1 clove garlic
¼ cup minced onion
½ cup chopped celery
⅓ cup French Dressing*
Romaine lettuce
1 cup Mayonnaise*

Peel the eggplant, dice, and cook in water with lemon juice, salt, and garlic for about 5 minutes until barely tender. Mix with the onions, celery, and French Dressing. Let stand in the refrigerator for a couple of hours to bring out the flavor. Serve on the lettuce with Mayonnaise on the side.

### MEXICAN PINEAPPLE COCONUT SALAD
(*4 servings*)

1 cup cubed pineapple
1 cup grated coconut
2 cups shredded cabbage
1 cup Mayonnaise*
1 teaspoon lemon juice
Lettuce

Combine all ingredients, except lettuce, and toss gently. Chill, and serve on a bed of lettuce.

## CEVICHE
### (6 *servings*)

- 1 pound halibut or ½ pound any white fish and ½ pound scallops
- 1 cup lemon juice
- ½ cup chopped onions or scallions
- 1 cup tomato juice
- 1 teaspoon salt
- ½ teaspoon pepper
- 2 tablespoons Worcestershire sauce
- ½ (14 ounce) bottle tomato catsup
- ½ teaspoon Tabasco sauce
- ½ teaspoon oregano
- 2 tablespoons chopped parsley

Cut the raw fish into about ½ inch cubes and marinate in the lemon juice for at least one hour. Mix the onions, tomato juice, salt, pepper, Worcestershire sauce, catsup, Tabasco sauce, oregano and parsley. Pour off excess lemon juice from the fish and fold into the sauce. Adjust seasoning, adding a little of the lemon juice to taste. Let stand several hours or overnight.

## MEXICAN FRUIT SALAD
### (6–8 servings)

- 4 bananas
- 4 oranges
- 1 sweet pepper or pimento
- 3 tablespoons shredded coconut
- ¼ cup Fruit French Dressing*
- 1 teaspoon fresh mint or ¼ teaspoon dried

Cut the bananas once through lengthwise and then once in half making 16 pieces. Arrange the sectioned oranges and strips of pepper or pimento over the bananas. Add the dressing and let stand in refrigerator for about an hour. Sprinkle with mint.

# South American Salads

Corn, lima beans, avocados, tomatoes, and potatoes were all part of the "wealth of the Indies" which the conquistadors discovered in New Spain. They still enrich South American salads. Potatoes originated in Peru, and are almost a national dish there. They form one of the important ingredients in South American salads.

### PERUVIAN POTATO SALAD
### *PAPAS A LA HUANCAINA*
(6–8 *servings*)

2 pounds small new potatoes, boiled in jackets
½ pound Cheddar cheese, grated
4 yolks of hard boiled eggs
3 mashed chilies or 1 teaspoon chili powder
1 teaspoon salt
¼ teaspoon pepper
¼ cup olive oil
1 cup evaporated milk
½ teaspoon lemon juice
½ cup minced onion
Lettuce (garnish)
Olives (garnish)

Cool and peel the boiled potatoes. Place on the serving platter. Mash the cheese with the egg yolks, add the mashed chilies or chili powder, salt, and pepper, and beat well with a wooden spoon. Add the olive oil little by little, as in making mayonnaise. Add the milk and lemon juice. Add the minced onion, and adjust the seasoning to taste. Cover the potatoes with this sauce, and garnish with lettuce and olives. Serve cold.

## COLOMBIAN VEGETABLE SALAD
*(4–6 servings)*

3 Spanish style sausages, diced
½ cup cooked green beans
½ cup cooked corn
½ cup cooked lima beans
2 tomatoes, peeled and diced
1 small head lettuce
⅓ cup olive oil
⅓ cup vinegar
3 scallions, chopped
1 tablespoon minced parsley
1 clove garlic, crushed
1 teaspoon salt
¼ teaspoon pepper

Mix the sausage with the vegetables and lettuce torn into small pieces. Mix the rest of the ingredients and pour over. Toss, chill, and serve.

## SOUTH AMERICAN AVOCADO SALAD
*(6 servings)*

1 teaspoon salt
½ teaspoon freshly ground pepper
½ teaspoon sugar
2 tablespoons wine vinegar
¼ cup olive oil
1 clove garlic, minced
1 tablespoon minced chives or scallions
1 tablespoon minced parsley
1 tablespoon onion juice
1 head lettuce, shredded
2 avocados, peeled and diced

Mix the salt, pepper, and sugar. Add vinegar and oil and stir well. Add the garlic, chives, parsley, and onion juice, and mix well.

Add the lettuce and fold in the avocado. Do not cut the avocado until the dressing is ready or it will darken.

## VENEZUELAN AVOCADO AND SPINACH SALAD
### (4 servings)

½ pound spinach
2 tablespoons oil
2 onions, sliced thin
½ cup Mayonnaise*
1 large avocado
1 teaspoon lemon juice
2 hard boiled eggs
Lettuce

Put the spinach in a bowl and pour boiling water over it. Leave it for a few minutes only and then drain. Heat the oil, and sauté the onions for a few minutes until transparent but not brown. Put the spinach in a bowl with the onions. Add the Mayonnaise, peeled, diced avocado, lemon juice, and chopped egg. Chop all together until smooth, and serve on a bed of lettuce.

## BRAZILIAN AVOCADO SALAD
### (4 servings)

1 large clove garlic, minced
2 tablespoons minced onion
2 tablespoons chopped capers
2 tablespoons minced parsley
2 tablespoons minced chives
½ cup olive oil
3 tablespoons vinegar
1 teaspoon dry tarragon or 2 teaspoons fresh
1 teaspoon salt
¼ teaspoon pepper
1 large avocado
Salad greens

Mix all of the ingredients except the avocado and the greens. Wash and dry the salad greens and tear into pieces. You may use any kind of lettuce, endive, water cress, or a combination. Peel the avocado and slice thin. Combine the avocado and the greens and pour the salad dressing over. Toss gently and let stand for an hour.

# Russian Salads

There is no iron curtain in the salad world. Russian salads and Russian dressing appear all over. The only question is, what goes in it? Everybody has a different idea of *"Russki Salat."*

### RUSSIAN SALAD
*RUSSKI SALAT*
(*6–8 servings*)

2 cups diced cooked beef, veal, or chicken
½ cup cooked diced beets
½ cup diced pickles
½ cup diced cooked potatoes
1 cucumber, peeled and diced
2 hard boiled eggs, cut up
2 tablespoons chopped olives
1 cup sauerkraut
1 cup kidney beans
½ cup French Dressing*
½ teaspoon mustard

Use as many of the ingredients as possible. Do not omit the beets, pickles, or potatoes. Mix all of the vegetables together with the meat and add the French Dressing, which has been mixed with mustard. Toss thoroughly but gently.

## RUSSIAN HAM SALAD
### (8 *servings*)

3 cups diced ham
1 cup diced cooked potatoes
½ cup chopped onions
1 cup diced pickle
1 tablespoon capers
1 teaspoon lemon juice
2 tablespoons caviar
½ cup Mayonnaise*

Mix the ham, potatoes, onion, pickle, and capers. Add the lemon juice and caviar to the Mayonnaise. Fold into the meat and vegetable mixture.

## RUSSIAN VEGETABLE SALAD
### (6 *servings*)

4 carrots, cooked and diced
1 cup cooked diced green beans
1 cup cooked peas
2 medium potatoes, boiled in jackets
½ cup Mayonnaise*
2 tablespoons catsup or chili sauce
2 teaspoons lemon juice
2 tablespoons French Dressing*

Mix the carrots, green beans, and peas in a salad bowl. Peel and dice the potatoes and add to the other vegetables. Mix the Mayonnaise with catsup or chili sauce, lemon juice, and French Dressing. Toss gently into the vegetable mixture.

## SWEET PEPPER SALAD
### *SLADKY PEREZS*
#### (6–8 *servings*)

6 green or sweet red peppers, or 3 green and 3 red
1 teaspoon salt
¼ teaspoon pepper
2 teaspoons sugar
2 teaspoons prepared mustard
1–2 tablespoons vinegar
⅓ cup olive oil

Cut the pepper into eighths or quarters and boil in salted water for about 15 minutes until tender. Chill. Mix the salt, pepper, sugar, and mustard. Stir in 1 tablespoon vinegar and the oil. Add more vinegar to taste. Pour over the peppers and let stand for several hours.

# Near Eastern Salads

All around the Eastern Mediterranean, salad greens flourish under the sun. Here the olive and the oil of the olive reign supreme, while yogurt and mint add a distinctive fillip. A few ingredients in salads from the Arab world are not always available in supermarkets; however, native stores in almost all cities can supply such things as Greek fish roe or powdered or dried mint.

## GREEK SALAD
### (4 servings)

3 tomatoes, cut up
1 head lettuce, shredded
1 bunch radishes, sliced
1 cucumber, diced
¼ pound Greek cheese
16 pitted ripe olives
¼ cup French Dressing*

Mix the tomatoes, lettuce, radishes, and cucumbers. Add the cheese broken into small pieces and the cut up olives. Toss with the dressing.

## TARAMASALATA
### (8 servings—12 hors d'oeuvre servings)

½ pound Tarama or ½–¾ pound cod fish roe
4–5 slices white bread
1–1½ cups olive oil
Juice of 1–2 lemons
Thin toast or lettuce

If using salted Tarama, rinse it in cold water, letting it stand about 15 minutes. Drain through cheese cloth or a fine mesh sieve. If you use fresh roe parboil it in heavily salted water and pull off any membrane. Cut crusts off the bread, wet it and squeeze dry. Add the bread to the roe in a bowl and mix. Stir steadily while adding the oil in a very slow stream. This is made as you would make mayonnaise and should be fluffy and light when finished. Add lemon juice to taste. Serve with thin toast or on lettuce leaves.

## TURKISH CUCUMBER SALAD
### (4 *servings*)

1 large cucumber, grated
1 cup yogurt
2 tablespoons blanched white raisins
2 tablespoons chopped walnuts
1 small onion, minced
½ teaspoon salt
¼ teaspoon pepper
1 teaspoon chopped mint

Combine all of the ingredients. Chill.

## ARMENIAN EGGPLANT SALAD
### (6 *servings*)

1 eggplant
1 medium onion, chopped
2 tablespoons minced parsley
1 teaspoon salt
½ teaspoon pepper
¼ cup oil
⅓ cup vinegar
Lettuce
Tomatoes (garnish)
Ripe olives (garnish)

Bake, broil, or boil the eggplant until soft. Cool, peel and chop. Mix the eggplant with onion and parsley. Add salt and pepper, and mixture of the oil and vinegar. Toss. Serve on lettuce and garnish with tomato wedges and pitted ripe olives.

### ARMENIAN COLE SLAW
#### (6–8 servings)

- 1 head cabbage, chopped fine
- 2 large cooked beets, chopped
- 1 large green pepper, chopped
- 1 cup Mayonnaise*
- 2 tablespoons vinegar
- 2 tablespoons sugar

Mix the cabbage, beets, and green pepper. Thin the Mayonnaise with vinegar and add the sugar. Mix into the salad, tossing thoroughly.

## MOROCCAN CUCUMBER SALAD
### (*4 servings*)

2 large cucumbers
3 tablespoons vinegar
1 clove garlic, crushed
1 tablespoon soy sauce
1 teaspoon sesame oil

Do not peel the cucumbers. Score them lengthwise with the
prongs of a fork before slicing thin if you wish. Put the cucumbers in a bowl with vinegar, garlic, and soy sauce, and let stand
several hours in the refrigerator. Stir in the sesame oil just before
serving.

## CRACKED WHEAT AND PARSLEY SALAD
### *TABBOULEH*
### (*6 servings*)

1 cup burghot (wheat pilaf)
1 bunch green onions, chopped fine
1 teaspoon salt
½ teaspoon pepper
½ cup chopped fresh mint or 2 tablespoons dried
1½ cups chopped parsley
½ cup olive oil
½ cup lemon juice
2–3 large tomatoes, peeled and chopped
Lettuce

Pour 1 cup boiling water over the burghot and let stand until water is absorbed, about half an hour. Squeeze dry between hands.
Mix with onions, salt, and pepper, crushing the onions into the
burghot. Stir in parsley and mint. Add the oil and lemon juice
and taste for seasoning. Stir in half of the tomatoes and put the
rest on the platter or put all on the platter. Serve the salad on

lettuce and if you wish to "go native," provide vine or cabbage leaves to use as scoops to eat with.

### LEBANESE POTATO SALAD
*(4 servings)*

1 pound potatoes, boiled in jackets
¼ cup oil
¼ cup lemon juice or vinegar
1 clove garlic, crushed
1 teaspoon salt
¼ teaspoon pepper
2 tablespoons chopped scallions
2 tablespoons chopped parsley

Peel and slice the boiled potatoes thin. Add a mixture of oil, lemon juice or vinegar, garlic, salt, and pepper while the potatoes are still warm. Add scallions and 1 tablespoon parsley and toss gently. Garnish top with remaining parsley.

### PERSIAN SPINACH SALAD
### *BORANI ESFANAJ*
*(4 servings)*

1 pound spinach
1 onion, minced
1 tablespoon oil
2 cups yogurt
1 teaspoon salt
¼ teaspoon pepper
2 cloves garlic, crushed
1 teaspoon fresh mint or ½ teaspoon powdered
2 tablespoons chopped walnuts

Cut up the spinach and combine with onion. Cook only in the water which clings to the spinach after washing. Cook 3 minutes. Drain. Add oil and cook 2 more minutes. Remove from heat, cool. Add the yogurt, salt, pepper, and garlic. Top with mint and nuts.

## PERSIAN CUCUMBER SALAD
### (6 servings)

2 cucumbers, grated
2 cups yogurt
2 tablespoons white raisins, plumped
2 tablespoons chopped walnuts
1 onion, minced
½ teaspoon salt
¼ teaspoon pepper
¼ teaspoon powdered mint
¼ teaspoon dried marjoram or basil

Mix the drained cucumbers with yogurt and add the remaining ingredients. Chill. Raisins are plumped by bringing just to a boil, or leaving in water for an hour.

# Oriental Salads

As I learned the hard way in Hong Kong, the inscrutable Oriental adds his mystery touch of curry, ginger, sesame, or soy to his characteristic bean sprouts, peppers, and greens. From Singapore to Rangoon, from Yokohama to Bombay, the salads are redolent of the East, with their unmistakable flavor, intriguing and delightful.

### SINGAPORE CHICKEN SALAD
### (6 *servings*)

1  4 pound frying chicken
⅓  cup sherry or saki
⅓  cup soy sauce
1½  teaspoons minced fresh ginger or ½ teaspoon powdered
3  tablespoons oil
1  cup bean sprouts
1  cup diced celery
1  tablespoon sesame seeds
2  cups shredded lettuce
½  cup sliced almonds

Cut the chicken off of the bones into bite-size pieces. Marinate in a mixture of sherry or saki, soy sauce, and ginger for several hours. Reserve marinade. Brown the chicken in the oil. Add ⅓ cup of water and the remaining marinade. Cover and simmer for about 15 minutes until the chicken is tender. Cool. Mix the remaining ingredients. Pour over the chicken and mix thoroughly. Adjust the seasoning to taste.

## INDIAN CUCUMBER SALAD
(*4 servings*)

2 cucumbers
2 tablespoons salt
1 tablespoon peanut oil
1 tablespoon sesame oil
1 tablespoon vinegar
1 teaspoon sugar
1 teaspoon curry
1 tablespoon soy sauce
1 clove garlic, crushed

Shred the peeled cucumbers, and sprinkle with salt. Let stand for several hours. Put in a strainer and let cold water run over them. Drain. Put into a bowl with all of the ingredients and let stand at least 2 hours in refrigerator.

## BANGKOK SHRIMP SALAD
(*6 servings*)

2 pounds shrimp
1 bay leaf
1 tablespoon salt
½ tablespoon peppercorns
¼ cup minced shallots
2 cloves garlic, crushed or minced
3 tablespoons olive oil
½ cup minced green peppers
1 apple, minced or grated
3 tablespoons chopped peanuts
2 tablespoons soy sauce
1 cup coconut milk or ¾ cup milk and ¼ cup moist coconut
Lettuce

Simmer the shrimp in water with the bay leaf, salt, and peppercorns for 5 minutes. Drain, cool, peel, and devein, and cut the shrimp once through lengthwise. If they are large, cut once or twice across. Sauté the shallots and garlic in olive oil until they are transparent but not brown. Cool and mix with the remaining ingredients. Pour this over the shrimp and serve on shredded lettuce.

## RANGOON SHRIMP SALAD
### (6 servings)

- 2 pounds shrimp
- 1 tablespoon salt
- 1 tablespoon coarsely ground pepper
- 1 cup chopped scallions
- ½ teaspoon dried chili peppers
- 4 tablespoons lime or lemon juice
- 1 tablespoon soy sauce

Bring the shrimp to a boil in water with the salt and pepper. Cook for 3 minutes after the water comes to a boil. Cool, peel, and devein the shrimp, and cut into large dice. Mix with the scallions and chili peppers, and sprinkle with the mixture of lime or lemon juice and the soy sauce.

## CAMBODIAN AVOCADO LITCHI SALAD
### (12 servings)

- 6 avocados
- ¼ cup lemon juice
- 1 (1 pound 4 ounce) can litchi nuts
- ¼ cup oil
- 2 tablespoons soy sauce
- 2 teaspoons grated fresh ginger
- Lettuce (optional)

Cut the avocados in half—do not peel. Sprinkle cut surfaces with 2 tablespoons of lemon juice. Drain the nuts and save the liquid. Put the nuts in a bowl with remaining lemon juice, oil, soy, and ginger. Add 3 tablespoons of liquid to the nuts. Stir and fill the avocados with this mixture. Serve on shredded lettuce, if you wish. When you are in Cambodia, make the salad with fresh ripe litchis!

## JAPANESE TURNIPS AND CARROTS
### (6 servings)

4 cups thinly sliced turnips
1 cup thinly sliced carrots
2 tablespoons salt
½ cup vinegar
2 tablespoons sugar
¼ teaspoon Ajinomoto or MSG
½ teaspoon grated fresh ginger (optional)

Sprinkle the turnips and carrots with salt and let stand for an hour. Rinse and press out moisture. Mix the vinegar, sugar, Ajinomoto or MSG, and the ginger, if you wish, and pour over the salad. Chill and serve.

## JAPANESE MARINATED MUSHROOMS
### (8 servings—12–15 canapé servings)

1 pound small mushrooms
2 tablespoons soy sauce
¼ cup saki or sherry
3 tablespoons vinegar
2 tablespoons minced onion
1 tablespoon sugar
1 teaspoon salt

Remove the stems from the mushrooms, and unless the caps are pure white, peel them. Mix the soy with the wine, vinegar, onion, sugar, and salt, and bring to a boil. Pour hot over the mushrooms. Refrigerate for a day or two turning the mushrooms once or twice.

SALAD DAYS AROUND THE GLOBE

## CHINESE ASPARAGUS SALAD
### (4 servings)

2 pounds asparagus
2 tablespoons soy sauce
1 tablespoon sesame or olive oil
½ teaspoon sugar
Salad greens (optional)

Cut the green part of the asparagus in 1 inch pieces diagonally.
Cook in boiling salted water for 3 minutes only. Drain and chill.
Mix the soy sauce, oil, and sugar. Marinate the asparagus in this
for at least 1 hour in refrigerator. Serve on greens if you wish.

## CHINESE FISH SALAD
### (8 servings)

3–4 pounds pike, tuna, or other very fresh fish
2 tablespoons lemon juice
4 carrots, shredded
1 large or 2 small dill pickles, minced
2 tablespoons peanuts, pounded fine
1 teaspoon grated fresh ginger or ½ teaspoon powdered
1 teaspoon salt
1 tablespoon vinegar
¼ cup olive or salad oil
1 tablespoon toasted sesame seeds (optional)

Remove any skin and bones from fish and cut in very thin slices.
Sprinkle with lemon juice. Add the carrots, pickles, and nuts. Mix
in ginger, salt, vinegar, oil, and sesame seeds, if you wish, and pour
over the fish. Let stand in refrigerator several hours.

## CHINESE CUCUMBER SALAD
### *LIANG PAN HUANG KUA*
(*4 servings*)

2 cucumbers
3 tablespoons vinegar
¼ cup light soy sauce
1 tablespoon sugar
1 teaspoon MSG
3 tablespoons sesame seed oil

Slice the unpeeled cucumbers paper thin. Add the other ingredients except the oil. Let marinate for several hours, then add the oil and stir. Chill.

## CHINESE TUNA SALAD
(6 *servings*)

2 (7 ounce) cans tuna
1 cup chopped scallions
1 cup chopped celery
¼ cup diced green pepper
2 cups bean sprouts
¾ cup Mayonnaise*
2 tablespoons soy sauce
Lettuce

Break up the tuna, and toss gently with the scallions, celery, green pepper, and bean sprouts. If using canned sprouts, drain them. Mix the Mayonnaise and soy sauce, and fold into the salad. Serve on lettuce.

## CHINESE CHICKEN SALAD
### (6 servings)

1½  cups coarsely cut celery
3  cups cut up cooked chicken
3  tablespoons olive oil
3  tablespoons soy sauce
¼  teaspoon pepper
Pinch sugar
Lettuce (optional)

Put celery in warm water. Bring to a boil and cook for 3 minutes.
Drain and cool. Mix with the chicken. Pour over a mixture of the
oil, soy sauce, pepper, and sugar. Serve on lettuce, if you wish.

# Chapter Four

## WHAT THE WELL-DRESSED SALAD WILL WEAR

Variety is the spice of salad making, and is attained most easily by varying the dressing. There are so many kinds and varieties of dressing, and each has its own place in the range of salads.

First off, you ask yourself: What do I want to highlight, the salad or the dressing? If you wish to snap up the taste of simple greens, you may decide to use a high-flavored dressing, like Roquefort. Chicken salad, however, must taste of chicken, so you will probably thin your mayonnaise with strong chicken broth. To potatoes, which are mild, you will add some member of the onion family to give character to the blend.

Dressing a salad, like dressing a pretty girl, is not an exact science; it is an art. Your own imagination is the extra ingredient that makes menu magic.

My imagination and my long experience have gone into the recipes which follow; but your fancy must add to, subtract from, or vary, the listed ingredients. These recipes are here to suggest; you will improvise upon them.

When I say "Season to taste" I always mean "Taste to season." Don't overpower the blend by tossing in the whole quantity of anything at once. You may like it better with less.

How big is "a pinch?" As big as you like it. It doesn't depend on the size of your fingers; it depends on your palate. As you try these recipes, start with a scanty pinch, and add if you please. Once the seasoning is in, you can't take it out; but you can add more, a bit at a time, *ad infinitum* (but please, never *ad nauseam!*).

It is so satisfying to blend your own dressings with your own individual imagination, that under normal circumstances it is a shame to buy commercial mixtures. Good ingredients which you mix yourself exactly to your own taste give you the best of dressings, and cost less than ready-mixed preparations at the market.

If you are in a hurry, and must use a "boughten" dressing, make haste slowly. Commercial dressings, on supermarket shelves as on restaurant tables, are more over-salted, over-peppered, over-sugared, over-spiced, over-garlicked with stale garlic, than any other product. Choose a dressing that is not flavored to death, and add your own personal taste touch to it. A pinch of curry (*not* a spoonful) will add an elusive tang to any oil and vinegar dressing. A little more curry, or some dill, added to Best Foods (Hellmann's) Mayonnaise, suits the shrimp salad, as *fines herbes* make a green mayonnaise to compliment the salmon.

The best mayonnaise is made in your kitchen. It takes so little time, it's easy to make and tastes so good. All you need in addition to the egg yolks, oil, and either lemon juice or vinegar (at room temperature please) is a fork or whip, a bowl, and a little patience at the beginning. The secret of handmade mayonnaise is the very slow, almost drop by drop, addition of oil to the egg yolks while stirring. After this thickens you can add the oil in a thin stream, watching to see that it is absorbed into the mixture. A cup of mayonnaise should not take more than ten minutes to make.

Blender mayonnaise is faster—about three minutes total time. Put the whole egg with vinegar or lemon juice into the blender, turn it on at low speed and pour in the oil in a steady stream.

You can add flavors to the mayonnaise after it is done: minced parsley or chives, curry, herbs, mustard, pepper, paprika, caraway seeds, capers, or whatever.

Mixing a French salad dressing is one of the easiest of the civilized arts. If you use a glass jar with a cover, it is easiest of all. Condiments go in first, salt and pepper and whatever else is to be used. Add a spoonful of water to dissolve the salt. Next add the vinegar, then the oil. Cover the jar and give it a good shake. Presto! Your salad dressing is mixed.

You don't even need to obey the old adage by calling in a miser to add the vinegar, a spendthrift to pour the oil, and a madman to shake up the whole. You can do it all yourself.

The glass jar technique has many advantages over stirring up the ingredients in a bowl. The dressing can be made ahead, and shaken again to attain the proper consistency at the last moment. You can make a superfluity, and what is left for tomorrow can be stored away in the same jar.

A trick to thicken the oil and mellow the vinegar is to add an ice cube to the mixture just before you shake it. Shake it with a flourish, as if you were shaking a cocktail.

The fine art of mixing a salad dressing reaches its apogee when you do it in public. Then it becomes a production. The guests around the table are your audience.

To set the stage, you assemble your properties. You must have cruets of oil and vinegar to decant with a flourish. If you are using a fancy vinegar, never mind the cruet. Keep it in the original bottle for the guests to admire. At hand you will also have the pepper-grinder, and a saltcellar for pinches or a shaker for sprinkles, together with a little sugar. With these properties at your elbow and no others, you can compound a delicious French dressing.

Now, if you want to gild the lily, you will have to set out a selection of other ingredients, such as mustard, curry, paprika, or Worcestershire sauce, flanked by herbs, dried or fresh, minced scallions or chives, or garlic in a press. The crowning touch is ready in a topping like croutons, minced egg, crumbled bacon, anchovies, or grated cheese.

Don't go overboard in assembling your properties. You are not whipping up short orders. Lay out only the few interesting ingredients you have chosen to blend into your salad dressing.

The properties are assembled. The curtain rises. The mixing magic begins. With a few mystic passes you mix the dressing, with a fork in a handy saucer, or directly over the salad bowl full of greens.

Now comes the grand gesture, the climax of the drama, as you toss and tumble the greens till every mouthful is lightly coated with the good taste of your original dressing creation.

If you want the flourish of tossing at the table, without the delay of measuring and mixing the ingredients for the dressing, you can make your mixture in the kitchen, compounding it in the bottom of the salad bowl. Then cross the salad fork and spoon over it, gently pile the greens above, and chill till the moment arrives for mixing all together at the table. This ensures keeping the greens crisp and dry till tossing time comes.

I remember how Oscar of the Waldorf used to mix the salad for Father and me, lunching at the table in his private dining room in the hotel. He would compound enough dressing for the three of us, right into the big salad spoon, holding it over the bowl of greens.

He would start with a sprinkle of salt and pepper, adding a little water to dissolve it. Next, in went the vinegar sparingly, the oil generously, overflowing into the salad. Then he would toss. He was always careful not to get his greens too wet with dressing. It was a delight to watch the expansive old gentleman, his fine features gleaming with the joy of an artist, as he poured and mixed, and to anticipate the pleasure of tasting his delicate, subtle concoction.

In a dressing of such elegant simplicity, of course Oscar used only the most precious ingredients: *olive* oil and *wine* vinegar. Olive oil is the most ancient as well as the best of all oils. Perhaps it was known first in Bible lands. The Homeric Greek warriors rubbed themselves down with it. It was the Greeks who introduced it into Italy, where it has lived happily ever after.

Olive oil comes from green olives pressed in a vat. The lightest of the oil, rising to the top, is the best grade, romantically called "virgin." The heavier oil, lying in lower layers, is graded as less desirable. The lightest of all olive oil is produced by the French. Olive oil from Italy, slightly heavier, is imported in abundance.

Don't suppose that olive oil forms the only basis of a good salad dressing. Other very acceptable oils are made from corn, peanuts, cotton-seed, soybeans, and safflower, which produce bland oils of very little flavor. These salad oils are much less expensive than olive oil, and it is good economy to mix olive and salad oil in a dressing if the olive taste is wanted, or to use all salad oil in a high-flavored dressing.

With oil, from ancient times, comes vinegar. Medieval alchemists conjured with vinegar. Four hundred years ago Sir Thomas Elyot opined in *The Castel of Helth* that "olyves doth corroborate the stomake, being eaten with vinegar"; and not long afterward, King James I of England called for "winiger to his sallet."

Undoubtedly, what they brought to the King's table was the regal distillation, wine vinegar. In most of Europe, vinegar from white or red wine is still the rule. However, in America today cider vinegar, or a white vinegar, is cheaper and very satisfactory for dressing a salad.

More than one vinegar is needed on every kitchen shelf. You will probably stock both wine and cider vinegar. In addition, you may choose an herb vinegar, flavored with some herb like tarragon or basil, or an exotic vinegar such as pear. Varying the vinegar is one good way to change the taste of your salads.

Another easy means to salad variety is found on your shelf of herbs and spices.

# Herbs for Salads

Fresh herbs are much the best. When using dried you need about a third as much as the fresh ones.

*BASIL Aromatic and tangy, basil has a special affinity for tomatoes; also use with seafood, cucumbers, beans, potatoes, and greens.

BAY LEAF (*Laurel*) Strong almost bitter taste, used frequently in French cookery; good in marinades and for beets and artichokes.

BORAGE Fresh young leaves are a splendid addition to greens.

BURNET A cucumber-flavored herb, good with vegetables.

CAPERS The salty taste whets the appetite, so use with first-course salads and on poultry, meat, fish, and tomatoes.

DILL Use the feathery leaves and minced tender tips of stems in seafood and with cucumbers, potato salad, and cole slaw.

FENNEL Bulb and some of the feathery foliage will add a licorice flavor. Slice the bulb into mixed and vegetable salads.

LOVAGE This parsley-family herb has a strong celery flavor; use sparingly.

*MARJORAM (*Sweet Marjoram*) A delightful herb which blends well with most salads—poultry, eggs, cole slaw, tomatoes, spinach, and other vegetables.

MINT A lively taste; use sparingly with fruits, cole slaw, carrots, beans, and beets.

NASTURTIUM Flowers as well as leaves add beauty and a spice taste to green and mixed salads.

*ONION FAMILY (*Chives, garlic, onions, leeks, scallions, and shallots*) The most used of all—use in one form or another, always in potato salad and in most salads and salad dressings. Onions and garlic are available as pungent powder, as salt, and minced. Chives are available minced, dried, or frozen.

OREGANO   (*Wild Marjoram*)  Used in most Italian and Spanish recipes. A potent herb, use carefully with tomatoes, potato salad, spinach, greens, and seafood.

*PARSLEY   A universally popular herb. There are two varieties, curly and flat leaf. Use freely in all salads except fruit and desserts.

ROSEMARY   A fragrant herb to be used cautiously with greens and vegetables, especially spinach and potatoes. Good in meat salads.

SAVORY   (*Summer Savory and Winter Savory*)  Sometimes called "the bean herb." Use summer savory in any green and vegetable salads. Winter savory is particularly good with beans and peas.

SORREL   This has a slightly sour taste; use young leaves in mixed greens.

*TARRAGON   An unusual fascinating flavor, used often in vinegars, good with almost all salads.

THYME   Unexpectedly good if used sparingly in vegetable and meat salads.

WOODRUFF   Famous as a flavor in May Wine, try it on fruits.

*FINES HERBES   Are a combination of parsley, tarragon, chervil, and chives. Don't mix your own; buy a blend from a reputable herb grower.

*BLENDED SALAD HERBS   Are a most useful jar on your shelf. A good herb farm is better able to combine these than you are!

* Denotes the most important herbs for salads.

# Spices and Seeds for Salads

Keep spices in tightly sealed jars, grind or grate them yourself when possible. Buy small quantities; they lose their flavor.

ALLSPICE   The pungent berry of a tree used to flavor vinegar and in cole slaw and spicy fruits.

CARAWAY SEEDS   Aromatic seeds for cabbage and potato salads.

CARDAMOM SEEDS   Ground or whole, these are delicious in fruit salads.

CAYENNE   (*Cayenne pepper*) Powder made from peppers—very useful in salad dressings.

CELERY SEEDS   Use this whenever you want a celery flavor; also available as celery salt.

CHILI POWDER   Ground from chili peppers. This distinctive flavor adds to vegetable, egg, and seafood salads.

CLOVE   This "spice nail" is available whole or ground; it is a most pungent spice—try a little on fruit for a change.

CURRY POWDER   A blend of a number of spices which takes its gold color from tumeric. It adds an exotic taste to seafood, poultry, and potato salads. A pinch or two in French dressing or mayonnaise enhances their flavor.

HORSERADISH   The young tender leaves add zest to a green salad. Prepared horseradish root is good in dressing for seafood.

*MUSTARD   Dry or prepared (wet) must be kept on your shelf; it may be used in almost any salad dressing. An invaluable spice.

NUTMEG   This large oval seed is much more pungent when freshly grated than when purchased in powdered form. Try a very little of this warm rather sweet spice on greens, cabbage, or fruit salads.

*PAPRIKA   This bright red powder (preferably from Hungary) adds color as well as a pungent flavor. Use in dressings and as a garnish on vegetables and other salads.

*PEPPER   Black pepper is used on almost any salad or salad dressing. White pepper, which is the same seed, with the outside coating removed, is slightly milder and preferable for fruit salad and some mayonnaises when you don't want to see black specks. Both peppers are available as peppercorns to be ground in pepper grinders in the kitchen or at table; pepper is also available in fine or coarse grinds.

POPPY SEEDS   These tiny seeds add texture as well as taste to cole slaw and fruit salads.

* Denotes the spices most useful in salads.

# SALADS

A list of frequently made salads and suggestions for appropriate herbs and spices. Remember minced parsley and minced scallions or chives help most salads except fruit and dessert. Mustard may be used in most salad dressings along with pepper and often paprika.

BEETS   Thyme, dill, chervil, bay

COLE SLAW   Thyme, marjoram, basil, mint, caraway seeds, poppy seeds, allspice, nutmeg

CUCUMBER   Dill, chervil, basil, borage, tarragon, cayenne

EGG   Marjoram, dill, *fines herbes*, curry, chili, celery seeds

FISH AND SHELLFISH   Dill, basil, oregano, thyme, capers, dry tarragon, curry, chili, celery seeds

FRUIT   Mint, woodruff, allspice, clove, nutmeg, poppy seeds, cardamom seeds, cayenne, paprika

GREEN   Tarragon, basil, chervil, marjoram, thyme, fennel, blended salad herbs

MEAT   Rosemary, thyme, tarragon, curry, chervil, dill, basil, horseradish

POTATO   Savory, basil, dill, chervil, rosemary, capers, oregano, caraway seeds, celery seeds, curry, onions in some form

POULTRY   Marjoram, tarragon, rosemary, thyme, fennel, capers,
curry, poppy seeds

TOMATOES   Basil, thyme, oregano, dill, marjoram, tarragon, savory,
chervil, capers

VEGETABLES   Thyme, marjoram, basil, tarragon, dill, savory, oregano, chervil, fennel, rosemary, lovage, burnet, celery seeds

Unless you are an expert, I would advise using herb blends put
up by reputable herb farms, which really understand which herbs
are allies, not enemies, complementing one another instead of
warring. For example, a knowing *fines herbes* mixture presents the
correct proportions of the right herbs. An Italian blend knows
how to give that real Roman flavor. "Mixed salad herbs" taste
different under different labels, but each goes well in a salad.

Spices have been and still are worth ten times their weight in
gold to the cook. The Queen of Sheba loaded her camels with
princely gifts of spices when she paid King Solomon a call. In
search of spices, Marco Polo caravaned to China, and Christopher
Columbus stumbled across America.

# French Dressing and Variations

On many a fancy Frenchified menu—*not* in France—I have read (trying to keep a straight face) such redundancies as:

> *Fromage de Brie cheese*
> *Coq au vin with wine sauce*
> *Roast beef with au jus*

A Frenchman would be equally mystified by encountering

> *Green salad with French dressing*

What else, he would wonder, would any gourmet in his senses put on a green salad? People from France would blush at the red dressings currently passing for French. If you want a real French French dressing, you had better make it yourself.

### BASIC FRENCH DRESSING
#### (*yields 1⅓ cups*)

⅓ cup wine or cider vinegar
¾ teaspoon salt
¼ teaspoon freshly ground pepper
1 cup olive oil

Mix the vinegar, salt, and pepper, and stir well. Add the oil slowly while beating.

### FRENCH DRESSING II

¼ cup wine vinegar
1 teaspoon salt
⅛ teaspoon pepper
½ teaspoon sugar
¼ teaspoon paprika
½ teaspoon dry mustard
1 cup olive oil

Mix the vinegar with seasonings and add the oil slowly while beating; this may be made with salad oil in place of olive oil.

### VARIATIONS OF FRENCH DRESSING I OR II

To French Dressing*, add:
  Catsup French—add 1 tablespoon catsup
  Chili Sauce French—add 2 tablespoons chili sauce
  Chutney French—add 2 tablespoons chutney, cut up
  Curry French—add 2 teaspoons curry
  Caper French—add 1 tablespoon capers
  Chive French—add 2 teaspoons minced chives
  Parsley French—add 1–2 tablespoons minced parsley
  Herb French—add 1–2 tablespoons minced fresh tarragon,
    chervil, basil, and/or chives or ¼–1 teaspoon dried

### FRENCH DRESSING III

½–1 teaspoon mustard
2 teaspoons salt
½ teaspoon pepper
½ teaspoon paprika
½ teaspoon sugar
½ teaspoon grated onion or 1 clove garlic (optional)
⅓ cup wine vinegar
1 tablespoon lemon juice (optional)
1 cup oil

Mix the dry ingredients and onion or garlic together. Add the vinegar, lemon juice, and then the oil. Shake well in a jar with an ice cube just before serving. Remove garlic. You may use a combination of olive and other salad oils if you wish.

## LEMON FRENCH DRESSING

3 tablespoons lemon juice
½ teaspoon salt
⅛ teaspoon pepper
¼ teaspoon sugar
¼ teaspoon dry mustard (optional)
½ cup olive oil or salad oil

Mix the lemon juice with salt, pepper, sugar, and mustard, if you wish. Then pour the oil in slowly, a teaspoon at a time.

## FRUIT FRENCH DRESSING

½ teaspoon salt
2–3 teaspoons sugar
¼ teaspoon dry mustard
¼ teaspoon curry powder
2 tablespoons lemon juice
2 tablespoons grapefruit or orange juice
⅔ cup oil

Mix the dry ingredients. Add fruit juice and mix well. Pour in the oil slowly while stirring. Good with citrus and other fruits.

## GARLIC FRENCH DRESSING

1 clove garlic, crushed
1 teaspoon salt
½ teaspoon freshly ground pepper
1 cup olive or salad oil
⅓ cup vinegar

Mix the ingredients in a jar and shake thoroughly before using.

## EGG AND OLIVE FRENCH DRESSING

1 cup French Dressing*
2 hard boiled eggs, chopped
1 tablespoon pitted or pimento stuffed olives, chopped

Blend all of the ingredients together. Excellent for mixed greens.


## HERB WINE FRENCH DRESSING

½ teaspoon salt
⅛ teaspoon white pepper
1 teaspoon sugar
¼ teaspoon dry mustard
½ cup white wine
1 teaspoon grated onion or 1 tablespoon minced shallots
¼ cup white wine vinegar
½ cup oil

Mix the dry ingredients. Stir in the wine, then add the grated onion, vinegar, and oil.


## INDIA FRENCH DRESSING

2 tablespoons chutney, chopped
½ teaspoon curry powder
1 cup French Dressing*

Add chutney and curry to the French Dressing, and mix. Good on fruit or meat salads.


## MUSTARD FRENCH DRESSING

½–1 cup French Dressing*
2 teaspoons prepared mustard (Dijon)
1 teaspoon grated onion
¼ teaspoon freshly ground pepper

Mix all of the ingredients thoroughly.

## SHERRY FRENCH DRESSING

1 teaspoon sugar
½ teaspoon salt
1 egg
¼ cup vinegar
1½ cups oil (½ olive)
½ cup sherry

Mix sugar, salt, and egg. Add the vinegar and then the oil slowly while beating. Add the sherry in a slow stream while stirring. Use part or all of a light French olive oil. Especially for a dessert salad.

## CREAMY PINK FRENCH DRESSING

1 cup French Dressing*
¼ cup catsup
1 egg white
1 tablespoon lemon juice

Put all of the ingredients together and beat with a rotary beater until fluffy. Try this for a change on mixed green salads.

## WATER CRESS FRENCH DRESSING
### LORENZO

1 cup French Dressing*
5 tablespoons water cress, chopped
¼ cup chili sauce
2 teaspoons Worcestershire sauce

Blend together. Use on mixed salads or lettuces.

## VINAIGRETTE

1 cup French Dressing*
2 tablespoons minced parsley
2 tablespoons minced pickle
2 tablespoons minced green pepper
2 tablespoons minced chives
1 tablespoon chopped capers (optional)

Combine all of the ingredients and shake to mix thoroughly. Recommended for asparagus.

## VINAIGRETTE II

¾ cup olive or salad oil or combination
¼ cup vinegar
1 teaspoon salt
¼ teaspoon pepper
1 teaspoon sugar
⅛ teaspoon paprika
1 teaspoon minced or grated onion
1 tablespoon minced parsley
3 tablespoons chopped dill pickle
1 hard boiled egg, grated

Mix the oil and vinegar with salt, pepper, sugar, and paprika. Beat, and then add the onion, parsley, and pickles while stirring. Stir in the grated egg.

## EGG VINAIGRETTE

2 hard boiled eggs
1 egg yolk
½ cup oil
1 teaspoon minced parsley
1 teaspoon minced oregano
1 teaspoon minced chives

1 teaspoon minced thyme
2 tablespoons lemon juice or vinegar
½ teaspoon salt
¼ teaspoon pepper

Mix mashed hard boiled egg yolks with the raw egg. Add oil a teaspoon at a time while beating. Add the rest of the ingredients and mix thoroughly. Stir in the egg white, chopped fine. Use this with an artichoke.

# Mayonnaise and Variations

Who's afraid of making mayonnaise? Nothing could be simpler than whipping up a bowlful.

The best mayonnaise is still made in your kitchen, with the yolk of an egg, some oil, a whisk or a fork, and some patience till the oil begins to take hold.

Have your ingredients at room temperature. Put the yolk in a bowl, add salt, a pinch or two of dry mustard if you wish, and then the oil, a very few drops at a time, stirring constantly. As the mixture thickens, you may add more oil in a thin, steady stream, continuing to stir. When the mayonnaise gets quite thick, thin it with a little lemon juice or vinegar, and then continue the slow addition of oil till you have made the quantity you desire.

Suppose it separates? Stop immediately. Start another yolk in another bowl, and be *sure* to add the oil very slowly, drop by drop, till it amalgamates. You may then use the separated mixture as you would oil. Nothing is lost or wasted.

Making mayonnaise in a blender is even quicker and easier, though perhaps a little less refined, as you use the whole egg.

Once you have made and served your own mayonnaise, you will want to make plenty, and serve it often, because it's so good, and so easy to make, and because it keeps so well. But if you want to keep it wholesome, be sure to keep it tightly covered in the refrigerator.

In choosing the oil for mayonnaise, it will depend on what you are going to use the mayonnaise for. If you use all olive oil, it makes a very pungent mayonnaise. Half olive oil and half of any blending oil, such as peanut or vegetable oil, makes a very useful dressing. You may use mostly a bland oil and flavor it with a small amount of olive oil if you wish.

## BASIC MAYONNAISE
### (*yields 1½ cups*)

1 egg yolk
½ teaspoon salt
¼–½ teaspoon dry mustard (optional)
1 cup oil
1–2 tablespoons vinegar or lemon juice

Mix the egg yolk, salt, and mustard if you wish together in the bottom of a bowl. Add the oil drop by drop while stirring. You may stir with a fork or rotary beater. When the mayonnaise begins to thicken, you may add the oil in a thin slow stream stirring constantly. If the mayonnaise gets too thick, add a little of the vinegar or lemon juice, and then continue the slow addition of oil.

## BASIC BLENDER MAYONNAISE
### (*yields 1¼ cups*)

1 egg
1 tablespoon wine vinegar or lemon juice
½ teaspoon salt
½ teaspoon dry mustard
¾ cup oil

Put the egg, vinegar or lemon juice, salt, and mustard in a blender. Add 2 tablespoons oil very slowly while the blender is at its lowest speed. Pour in the rest of the oil in a stream. The entire process of making the mayonnaise should not take more than a minute or two.

## MAYONNAISE VARIATIONS

To 1¼ to 1½ cups of Mayonnaise*, add any one of the following:
   ¾ cup chili sauce
   ⅛ teaspoon curry and ⅛ teaspoon paprika
   1 tablespoon French Dressing* and ½ teaspoon dry tarragon
   1 teaspoon curry and ½ teaspoon garlic salt
   2 teaspoons curry and 3–4 drops lemon juice
   2 teaspoons dry mustard and 1 teaspoon wine vinegar
   1 teaspoon lemon juice and 2 tablespoons broth

## CAPER MAYONNAISE

   1 cup Mayonnaise*
   2 tablespoons capers
   1 teaspoon grated onion
   ½ teaspoon poultry seasoning

Mix all of the ingredients together. The poultry seasoning may be omitted unless you are using the mayonnaise for poultry or cold veal salad.

## CARAWAY MAYONNAISE

   2 tablespoons vinegar
   1 tablespoon grated onion
   2 teaspoons caraway seeds
   1 teaspoon sugar
   ½ teaspoon salt
   ⅛ teaspoon pepper
   ½ cup Mayonnaise*

Mix all of the ingredients together with the Mayonnaise.

## CAVIAR MAYONNAISE

½ cup caviar
1 tablespoon onion or chives, chopped fine
1 tablespoon pimento, chopped
2 hard boiled eggs, chopped fine
1 teaspoon lemon juice
1 cup Mayonnaise*

Combine all of the ingredients with the Mayonnaise. For a special occasion use on soft greens or on any molded salad.

## RED CAVIAR MAYONNAISE

¼ cup red caviar
Juice ¼ lemon
1 tablespoon prepared horseradish
1 cup Mayonnaise*

Mix all of the ingredients except the Mayonnaise, and then stir that in very gently. Wonderful for egg salad.

## CHIVE MAYONNAISE

1 clove garlic
1 cup Mayonnaise*
3 tablespoons minced chives
1 tablespoon minced parsley
1 tablespoon minced pimento (optional)
¼ teaspoon freshly ground pepper

Rub a bowl thoroughly with the split clove of garlic. Mix the rest of the ingredients in the bowl. Good on tomato aspic.

## BLENDER GREEN MAYONNAISE

5 leaves spinach
1 tablespoon fresh tarragon or 1 teaspoon dry
1 tablespoon chopped chives or green onion
1 teaspoon chopped dill
1 teaspoon minced fresh marjoram or parsley
1 egg
½ teaspoon salt
½ teaspoon sugar
1 cup olive or salad oil or half and half
2 tablespoons tarragon or wine vinegar

Mix all of the ingredients except the oil and vinegar in a blender. Keep the blender at low speed and add half of the oil very slowly, then the vinegar, and then the remaining oil. Exceptionally good for salmon or tuna salads.

## GREEN GODDESS MAYONNAISE

2 tablespoons finely chopped anchovies or 1 tablespoon anchovy paste
3 tablespoons finely chopped chives or scallions
⅓ cup finely chopped parsley
½ cup heavy cream
1 tablespoon lemon juice
1 tablespoon tarragon vinegar
Dash of salt
Dash of freshly ground black pepper
1 cup Mayonnaise*

Mix all of the ingredients into the Mayonnaise, and let stand in the refrigerator for several hours to blend flavors. Use on crab or lobster salad, or any shellfish.

## GREEN GODDESS MAYONNAISE WITH SOUR CREAM

1 cup Mayonnaise*
1 cup sour cream
3 tablespoons tarragon vinegar, or 3 tablespoons vinegar and
   ½ teaspoon dried tarragon
1 tablespoon lemon juice
1 can anchovies
3 tablespoons chopped chives
¼ tablespoon chopped parsley
½ teaspoon salt
¼ teaspoon freshly ground pepper

Mix all of the ingredients together and put in a blender for 2 minutes, or beat with a rotary beater.

## GREEN MAYONNAISE

1 cup Mayonnaise*
1½ teaspoons chives, chopped fine
1 teaspoon tarragon leaves, chopped fine
1 tablespoon parsley, chopped fine
½ teaspoon chervil, chopped fine
½ teaspoon dill, chopped fine

Blend all together. Traditional on cold salmon, good on all fish salads.

## SHERRY MAYONNAISE

1 cup Mayonnaise*
¼ cup pale dry sherry
1 cup whipped cream

Mix all the ingredients together. Use on fruit salads, especially for dessert, also on chicken or turkey.

## SARDINE MAYONNAISE

1 cup Mayonnaise*
4 tablespoons mashed sardines
1 tablespoon chopped pimento
1 tablespoon onion, chopped fine
2 hard boiled eggs, chopped fine

Mix all together, let stand in refrigerator for several hours to blend flavors. A tasty dressing for greens.

## AVOCADO MAYONNAISE

1 medium-sized ripe avocado
1 tablespoon lemon juice
¼ cup Mayonnaise*
½ teaspoon salt
¼ teaspoon pepper
½ teaspoon chili powder
Pinch garlic powder
Pinch cayenne

Peel and mash the avocado with lemon juice until smooth, or buzz in a blender. Add Mayonnaise and all of the seasonings. Enhances any green salad.

## TARRAGON MAYONNAISE

1 cup Mayonnaise*
2 teaspoons tarragon vinegar
1 teaspoon lemon juice
2 tablespoons catsup
1 teaspoon dry tarragon or 3 teaspoons chopped fresh

Mix all together and let stand several hours. Marvelous for poultry salads.

## TARTARE SAUCE

1 cup Mayonnaise*
2 tablespoons finely chopped pickles
2 tablespoons finely chopped green olives
2 tablespoons finely chopped parsley
2 tablespoons coarsely chopped capers
2 tablespoons minced onion or chopped scallions

Mix all ingredients thoroughly. Use with fish.

## THOUSAND ISLAND DRESSING

1 cup Mayonnaise*
3 tablespoons chili sauce
1 tablespoon cider vinegar
1 tablespoon cream
1 tablespoon minced green pepper
¼ cup chopped celery
1 hard boiled egg, chopped fine
¼ teaspoon salt
½ teaspoon paprika

Mix all the ingredients very thoroughly.

# Cooked Dressings

For a less rich salad dressing, there is always a smooth, zesty cooked dressing. A cooked dressing is calorie-wise, because its basis is milk rather than oil. Cooked in a double boiler, it is smooth and bland and as tasty or rich as you care to make it. It tastes so good on cole slaw!

### COOKED DRESSING

1 teaspoon salt
¼ teaspoon white pepper
2 tablespoons sugar
½ cup flour
1 tablespoon mustard
1 cup milk
2 eggs
½ cup vinegar
1–2 tablespoons butter

Mix the dry ingredients. Add the milk and stir until smooth. Cook in a double boiler until thickened and smooth. Add the beaten eggs one at a time while cooking and heating. After 5 minutes, stir in the vinegar slowly. Remove from heat. Add a lump of butter, and stir well. Appropriate for cabbage salads.

### BOILED DRESSING

¼ cup cider vinegar
1 teaspoon salt
¼ teaspoon pepper
3 egg yolks
¼ cup cream

Heat the vinegar in a double boiler and add salt and pepper. Beat the egg yolks in a bowl and pour the warm vinegar over while stirring. Return to double boiler and cook and stir till creamy. Remove from heat and add the cream. Chill. For fruit or cole slaw. Serve with mousses and aspics.

### NOVA SCOTIA BOILED DRESSING

- 3 eggs, beaten
- 1 cup milk
- ¾ cup vinegar
- 2 tablespoons flour
- 2 tablespoons butter
- 1 teaspoon mustard
- ½ teaspoon salt
- ¼ teaspoon pepper

Heat the eggs and milk together. Heat the vinegar separately. Put the flour, butter, mustard, salt, and pepper in a bowl and stir in the hot milk. Cook until thickened and then add the warm vinegar. Use whenever you need a cooked dressing.

### COOKED OIL SALAD DRESSING

- 2 tablespoons flour
- 1 teaspoon sugar
- 3 tablespoons oil
- 1 teaspoon salt
- 2 eggs
- ¼ cup cider vinegar
- 2 teaspoons prepared mustard

Mix flour, sugar, oil, and salt with 1 cup of water. Heat until thickened. Mix the slightly beaten eggs with the vinegar and add slowly to the mixture while stirring. Cook and stir until quite thick. Add the mustard.

## COOKED FRUIT DRESSING

2 eggs
¼ cup sugar
⅓ cup lemon juice
2 teaspoons butter
⅛ teaspoon salt
2 tablespoons cream

Beat the eggs, add sugar, lemon juice, butter, and salt. Cook and stir until thick and fluffy. Cool. Just before serving, stir in the cream. Use on dessert salads. This is a sweet dressing.

## WHIPPED CREAM FRUIT DRESSING

1 tablespoon butter
¼ tablespoon sugar
1 egg
Juice 1 orange
Juice 1 lemon
½ cup heavy cream, whipped

Put butter, sugar, and the slightly beaten egg in a double boiler. Cook and stir until smooth and thick. Add fruit juices and mix. Cool and fold in the whipped cream. For any dessert salad.

## SHERRY DRESSING

1 egg, beaten
2 tablespoons sugar
¼ cup sherry
¼ teaspoon salt
2 teaspoons butter
¼ cup orange juice
2 tablespoons lemon juice
¼ cup heavy cream, whipped

Combine all ingredients except the cream in a double boiler. Cook until slightly thickened, stirring constantly. Chill. Fold in the whipped cream. Fine for fruits.

# Roquefort Dressings

Roquefort cheese makes salad taste different, according to how it is blended. You can enjoy it in French Dressing* or Mayonnaise*; or you might smooth it in white wine; or try it in sour cream or in olive oil. Any way you blend it, Roquefort is special!

### ROQUEFORT CHEESE DRESSING

¼ pound Roquefort cheese
¼ cup white wine
3 tablespoons olive oil
1 tablespoon lemon juice

Crumble the cheese and smooth it using the wine. Add the oil and lemon juice and mix thoroughly. Mixed greens are delicious with this flavorful dressing.

### ROQUEFORT FRENCH DRESSING

1 cup French Dressing*
¼ cup Roquefort or blue cheese

Crumble and cream the Roquefort cheese and then mix with the French Dressing. For mixed green salads, for a change.

### ROQUEFORT LEMON DRESSING

½ pound Roquefort cheese, crumbled
½ cup olive oil
¼ teaspoon pepper
Juice 2 lemons

Mash the cheese and olive oil until smooth. Add the pepper and lemon juice and stir well. For any salads where cheese flavor is appropriate, greens, fruit, tomatoes, etc.

### SOUR CREAM ROQUEFORT CHEESE DRESSING

1 cup sour cream
½ teaspoon salt
½ teaspoon dry mustard
½ teaspoon minced onion
⅛ pound Roquefort or blue cheese

Mix the cream, salt, mustard, and onion. Add to the crumbled Roquefort and stir until smooth. Use like any Roquefort dressing.

# Dairy Dressings

Cottage or cream cheese makes a smooth creamy dressing with or without the addition of heavy cream, especially if made in a mixer or blender. You may smooth the cheese with a little milk or half and half. Yogurt and cottage cheese are valuable for low-calorie dressings.

### CREAM CHEESE DRESSING

- 2 tablespoons Mayonnaise*
- 1 (3 ounce) package cream cheese
- ½ cup sour cream
- 1 tablespoon grated orange rind
- 1 tablespoon orange juice
- ¼ teaspoon salt

Blend the Mayonnaise into the cream cheese. Add the remaining ingredients and stir until mixed. Try with fruit or mixed salads.

### COTTAGE CHEESE DRESSING

- 1 cup cottage cheese
- ⅓ cup milk
- 1 teaspoon chopped chives or scallions
- 2 tablespoons chopped parsley
- ½ teaspoon salt
- ¼ teaspoon freshly ground pepper
- ½ teaspoon Worcestershire sauce

Whip the cottage cheese with the milk until creamy. Add remaining ingredients. Refrigerate for several hours. Try on tomato or cucumber salad, as well as green salads.

### COTTAGE CHEESE BUTTERMILK DRESSING

½ cup creamy cottage cheese
½ cup buttermilk
1 teaspoon salt
¼ teaspoon pepper
2 hard boiled egg yolks, mashed
1 tablespoon minced green pepper (optional)
1 tablespoon minced onion (optional)
1 teaspoon caraway seed (optional)

Mix all of the ingredients together very thoroughly. Use like other cottage cheese dressings.

### LOW-CALORIE COTTAGE CHEESE DRESSING

1 cup cottage cheese
½ cup buttermilk or skim milk
2–3 tablespoons wine vinegar
½ teaspoon grated onion
½ teaspoon salt

Combine the ingredients in a blender or mixer, or beat with a rotary mixer. Add a little artificial sweetener if this is to be used on fruit or dessert salad. About 2 calories per tablespoon.

### SOUR CREAM DRESSING

1 cup sour cream
1 tablespoon minced olives
¼ cup vinegar or ⅛ cup lemon juice
1 tablespoon sugar
1 teaspoon salt
¼ teaspoon pepper
1 tablespoon prepared horseradish
½ teaspoon mustard (optional)

Mix all of the ingredients together; let stand to blend flavors. Good for molds, mousses, and aspics.

## CAVIAR SOUR CREAM DRESSING

½ cup Mayonnaise*
½ cup sour cream
1 (2 ounce) jar black or red caviar
1 tablespoon catsup (optional)
¼ teaspoon grated onion
2 teaspoons lemon juice

Mix all of the ingredients together. A distinguished dressing for chicken or fish salads.

## YOGURT DRESSING

1 cup yogurt
1 teaspoon lemon juice
½ teaspoon finely minced chives
½ teaspoon salt
¼ teaspoon pepper
½ teaspoon paprika
½ teaspoon dry mustard

Combine the ingredients and mix until well blended. Chill. Use whenever you want a creamy dressing.

## CURRY YOGURT DRESSING

½ teaspoon salt
⅛ teaspoon paprika
⅛ teaspoon pepper
1 teaspoon sugar or 1 tablespoon honey
1–2 teaspoons curry powder
2 tablespoons lemon juice
1 pint yogurt

Mix all of the ingredients except the yogurt together and then stir in the yogurt. Good with fruit or poultry salads.

## YOGURT FRENCH DRESSING

½ cup Basic French Dressing*
1 cup yogurt
1 teaspoon celery salt
1 clove garlic, crushed (optional)

Mix all of the ingredients together. Use with mixed or fruit salads.

## LOW-CALORIE YOGURT DRESSING

1 cup yogurt
1 teaspoon salt
¼ teaspoon pepper
2 teaspoons prepared mustard
1 teaspoon salad herbs
1 teaspoon curry powder

Mix all of the ingredients gently together.

## YOGURT MINT LOW-CALORIE DRESSING

1 cup yogurt
2 tablespoons honey
2 tablespoons minced fresh mint or 2 teaspoons dried
2 teaspoons lemon juice

Mix all of the ingredients together and let stand to bring out the mint flavor. Reseason to taste. Only about 15 calories per tablespoon.

# Bonus Dressings

If you've gone along with me this far, you deserve a bonus, and here it is, in the mixed bag of out-of-the-ordinary, one-of-a-kind, super-delectable dressings that follow. There is no reason why you too can't develop your own blue-ribbon *bonus dressings!*

## SPECIAL SALAD DRESSING

1 clove garlic, crushed
½ teaspoon salt
¼ teaspoon pepper
⅛ teaspoon paprika
½ cup olive or salad oil or combination
1 egg
6 anchovies
¼ cup chopped water cress
3 tablespoons wine vinegar

Put the garlic in a bowl with salt, pepper, paprika, and mix. Add the oil slowly and the beaten raw egg. Mix the chopped anchovies, water cress, and vinegar, and beat in the oil mixture, and beat all together. Delicious!

## ALMOND GARLIC DRESSING

12 almonds
2 cloves garlic
1 teaspoon salt
¼ teaspoon white pepper
¾ cup olive oil
¼ cup wine vinegar

Crush the blanched almonds with garlic. Add the salt and pepper;

beat in the olive oil in a thin stream. Add the vinegar. Use on lettuce or mixed lettuces or greens.

## CREAMY AVOCADO DRESSING

1 cup mashed avocado
1 teaspoon lemon juice
½ teaspoon salt
2 tablespoons powdered sugar
1 teaspoon onion juice (optional)
1 cup heavy cream, whipped

Season the avocado with lemon juice, salt, sugar, and the onion juice, if you wish. Fold into the whipped cream. Use with greens or fruit.

## BACON DRESSING

6 slices bacon
½ cup vinegar
¼ teaspoon salt
½ teaspoon sugar
½ teaspoon pepper

Cook the bacon and remove from skillet. Add remaining ingredients to the bacon drippings. Heat. Crumble the bacon, and add to the dressing. Serve warm over lettuce or spinach for a wilted salad.

## CHICKEN LIVER DRESSING

½ pound chicken livers
2 tablespoons butter
1 medium onion, minced
4 hard boiled eggs
¼ cup Mayonnaise*
½ teaspoon salt
⅛ teaspoon pepper

Cook the livers in butter and add the onion. Reserve pan drippings. Chop the liver with the eggs. Add the pan drippings with the Mayonnaise and salt and pepper. Taste for seasoning. Serve on lettuce or mixed green salad.

### BELGIAN CREAM DRESSING

¼ cup olive oil
1 tablespoon lemon juice
⅓ cup heavy cream
1 teaspoon prepared mustard
1 tablespoon catsup
3 scallions or 1 small onion, minced
2 teaspoons minced parsley
½ teaspoon salt
¼ teaspoon vinegar

Mix all of the ingredients and shake thoroughly in a jar. Try on Belgian endive or other highly flavored greens.

### HORSERADISH HERB DRESSING

¾ cup sour cream
2 teaspoons tarragon or wine vinegar
2 tablespoons prepared horseradish
1 teaspoon sugar
⅛ teaspoon pepper
½ teaspoon salt
⅛ teaspoon paprika
1 teaspoon minced parsley
1 teaspoon minced dill or tarragon

Mix all of the ingredients together very thoroughly. This is a highly flavored dressing. Use for a change on appetizer salads and aspics.

## CUCUMBER SALAD DRESSING

1 cucumber, grated
1 tablespoon grated onion
1 cup sour cream
½ teaspoon salt
¼ teaspoon pepper

Combine all of the ingredients. Especially good with fish salads such as tuna or salmon.

## LEMON DRESSING

¼ cup lemon juice
¼ cup sugar
1 egg, well beaten
1 cup heavy cream, whipped

Combine the lemon juice, sugar, and egg in a double boiler. Cook until thick and smooth, stirring constantly. Chill. Fold in the whipped cream. Use with dessert salads.

## HONEY LEMON DRESSING

½ cup honey
1 teaspoon salt
1 teaspoon mustard
1 teaspoon paprika
½ cup lemon juice
1 cup salad oil

Mix all of the ingredients in a blender at low speed. Add the oil slowly while mixing. Appropriate for dessert salads, and fruit.

### LORENZO DRESSING

⅔ cup olive oil
⅓ cup vinegar
1 teaspoon salt
½ cup chili sauce
½ cup chopped water cress

Combine all the ingredients, and mix thoroughly. Wonderful on mixed salads of all kinds.

### MINT SALAD DRESSING

1 cup olive oil
¼ cup cider vinegar
1 tablespoon minced shallots or scallions
2 tablespoons minced fresh mint
1 teaspoon salt
¼ teaspoon pepper

Mix all of the ingredients together and shake or stir thoroughly. Good on fruit salads or mixed greens.

### MUSTARD DRESSING

1 tablespoon dry mustard
¼ cup dry white wine
1 egg yolk
½ cup salad oil
½ teaspoon salt
½ teaspoon sugar
1 clove garlic, crushed, or 1 teaspoon minced chives
2 teaspoons minced parsley

Mix all the ingredients together beating thoroughly. Add more mustard to taste. A strong dressing for a zesty salad.

## POPPY SEED DRESSING

½ cup sugar
1 teaspoon mustard
1½ teaspoons salt
⅓ cup vinegar
2 teaspoons onion juice (optional)
1 cup salad oil
2–3 tablespoons poppy seeds

Combine sugar, mustard, salt, vinegar, and onion juice. Put in blender or mixer at low speed and add oil in a very slow stream. You may make this with a rotary hand mixer beating steadily. Add poppy seeds. A sweet dressing for dessert.

## SPICY SALAD DRESSING

1 teaspoon dry mustard
½ teaspoon celery seed
½ teaspoon paprika
1 teaspoon salt
½ teaspoon freshly ground pepper
1 clove garlic crushed or ½ teaspoon garlic salt
⅓ cup cider vinegar
1 cup olive oil

Mix all of the dry ingredients together, and then add the vinegar and olive oil. A tasty dressing for vegetable salads.

## RED SALAD DRESSING

1 teaspoon salt
½ teaspoon pepper
½ teaspoon paprika
½ teaspoon mustard
1 teaspoon sugar
¼ cup vinegar

1 teaspoon Worcestershire sauce
Few drops Tabasco sauce
¾ cup salad oil (or part olive oil)
3 tablespoons chili sauce

Mix the dry ingredients. Stir in the vinegar, Worcestershire sauce, and Tabasco. Add the oil slowly while beating, and the chili sauce. Shake thoroughly in a bottle. Try this on shellfish.

## REMOULADE

1 teaspoon mustard
1 teaspoon anchovy paste
1 tablespoon vinegar
2 tablespoons sherry
½ clove garlic, crushed
3 tablespoons parsley
2–3 tablespoons capers
1 teaspoon onion juice or minced chives
1 cup Mayonnaise*

Mix all of the ingredients except Mayonnaise. Stir in the Mayonnaise. Let stand to blend flavors. Good with fish.

And if you aren't convinced by this time, there's no use telling you again

*SALAD IS GOOD*

# INDEX

Agg och Gurksallad, 125–26
Allspice, 160
Almond Garlic Dressing, 187–88
Almond Grape Salad, 96–97
Almonds, Chicken Salad with, 62
Anchovy and Cheese Salad, Swiss, 116
Anchovy Egg Salad, Scandinavian, 126
Anchovy Olive Salad, Spanish, 128
Apple Salads
  Celery and, 95
  Potato and, Austrian, 119
  Waldorf, 95
Applesauce Mold, Port, 102
Apricots with Liqueur, 100
Armenian Cole Slaw, 141
Armenian Eggplant Salad, 140–41
Artichokes, 48–49
  in Mustard Sauce, 49
Asparagus Salads
  Bean and, with Grapes, 43
  Chinese, 149
  Mousse, 86
  Vinaigrette, 44
Aspics, 81–86
  Cucumber, 84
  Ham, 85

Prune, 85
Tomato, 83
Tomato, Basic, 82
Tomato, Herbed, 82
Tongue in, 86
Vegetable, 84
Vegetables in, 83–84
Australian Lettuce, 26
Austrian Potato Apple Salad, 119
Austrian Red and White Cabbage Salad, 119
Avocado Dressing, Creamy, 188
Avocado Mayonnaise, 176
Avocados, 50
  Crab Salad in, 71
  Lobster Salad in, 72
  Shrimp Salad in, 74
Avocado Salad, 50–51
  Brazilian, 134–35
  Cambodian Litchi and, 147–48
  Cauliflower and, 46
  Citrus and, 51
  Filled, 51
  Grapefruit and, 92
    Molded, 89
    Persimmon, 92–93
  Litchi and, 147–48
  South American, 133–34
  Spinach and, 134

Avocado Salad (*cont'd*)
    Tomato and, 57–58
    Venezuelan Spinach and, 134

Bacon
    Salad Dressing, 188
    Spinach Salad with, 33
Bangkok Shrimp Salad, 146–47
Basil, 158
Bay Leaf, 158
Bean Salads
    Asparagus and, with Grapes,
        43
    Three or Four, 42–43
    Tomato and, French, 110
Beef Salad, 66–67
    Parisian, 109
    Russian, 136–37
    Tongue (*see* Tongue)
Beet (Beetroot) Salad, 44
    Appropriate Herbs, 161
    Fruit and, 45
    Mold, Swedish Pickled, 124
    Romaine and, 44
Belgian Cream Dressing, 189
Belgian Endive, 25
    Salads, 30–31
Bibb Lettuce, 25
Blended Salad Herbs, 159, 162
Blender Mayonnaise
    Basic, 171
    Green, 174
Boiled Dressing, 178–79
    Nova Scotia, 179
Bonus Dressings, 187–93
    Almond Garlic, 187–88
    Avocado, Creamy, 188
    Bacon, 188
    Chicken Liver, 188–89
    Cream, Belgian, 189
    Cucumber, 190
    Honey Lemon, 190
    Horseradish Herb, 189

    Lemon, 190
    Lemon Honey, 190
    Lorenzo, 191
    Mint, 191
    Mustard, 191
    Poppy Seed, 192
    Red, 192–93
    Remoulade, 193
    Special, 187
    Spicy, 192
Borage, 158
Borani Esfanaj, 143
Boston Lettuce, 25
Bouillabaisse Salad, 68–69
Bowls, Salad, 27–28
Brazilian Avocado Salad, 134–35
Broccoli Salad Vinaigrette, Ital-
        ian, 115
Broiled Grapefruit, 102–3
Bronze Lettuce, 25
Burghot and Parsley Salad, 142–
        43
Burnet, 158
Butter Lettuce, 25
Buttermilk   Cottage   Cheese
        Dressing, 184

Cabbage, 25
Cabbage Salad (Cole Slaw), 54
    Armenian, 141
    Austrian Red and White, 119
    German, 120
    Sour Cream, 54
Caesar Salad, 40
    California, 40–41
California Caesar Salad, 40–41
California Fruit Salad, 101
Cambodian   Avocado   Litchi
        Salad, 147–48
Cantaloupe   Salad. *See* Melon
        Salads
Caper French Dressing, 164
Caper Mayonnaise, 172

Capers, 158
Caraway Mayonnaise, 172
Caraway Seeds, 160
Cardamom Seeds, 160
Catsup French Dressing, 164
Cauliflower Salad, 45
  Avocado and, 46
Caviar Mayonnaise, 173
Caviar Sour Cream Dressing, 185
Cayenne, 161
Celery Root Salad, 47
  German (Knob Celery), 120
Celery Salad
  Apple and, 95
  Mushroom and, 56
  Orange and, 91
  Victor, 46
Celery Seeds, 160
Ceviche, 130
Cheese Dressings, 183–84
  Cottage, 183
    Buttermilk, 184
    Low-Calorie, 184
  Cream, 183
  Roquefort, 181–82
    French, 181
    Lemon, 181
    Sour Cream, 182
Cheese Salads. See also Chef's
    Salads
  Anchovy and Swiss, 116
  Cherries and Cream, 93
  Lemon Roquefort Mold, 88
  Macaroni Cheddar Salad Bowl,
    79
  Peach and, 94
  Pear and, 95
  Pineapple Mousse, 89
  Roquefort Mousse, 87–88
  Tuna and, 76–77
Chef's Salad Bowl, 37
Chef's Salads, 36–41
  Basic, 36

Caesar, 40–41
Chef's Salad Bowl, 37
Deviled Egg, 39
Salmon, 38–39
Shrimp, 38
Cherries and Cream Cheese, 93
Cherry Salad, 93
Chicken Liver Dressing, 188–89
Chicken Liver Salad, 64
Chicken Salads. See also Chef's
    Salads
  with Almonds, 62
  Appropriate Seasonings for
    Poultry, 162
  Chinese, 151
  Cobb, 65–66
  Corn and, 63
  with Cream Dressing, 63
  German, 121
  Liver, 64
  Mold, 63–64
  Russian, 136–37
  Singapore, 145
  Sunset, 65
Chick Pea Salad, 47
Chicory, 25
Chili Powder, 160
Chili Sauce French Dressing, 164
Chinese Asparagus Salad, 149
Chinese Chicken Salad, 151
Chinese Cucumbers, 150
Chinese Fish Salad, 149
Chive French Dressing, 164
Chive Mayonnaise, 174
Chives, 158, 161
Chutney French Dressing, 164
Citrus Avocado Salad, 51
Clams
  Bouillabaisse Salad with, 68–
    69
  Italian Seafood Salad with,
    112
Clove, 160

Cobb Salad, 65–66
Coconut Pineapple Salad, Mexican, 129
Cod Fish Roe, Taramasalata of, 139–40
Cod Salad, 69–70, 75
Cole Slaw (Cabbage Salad), 54
    Appropriate Seasonings, 161
    Armenian, 141
    Austrian Red and White, 119
    German, 120
    Sour Cream, 54
Colombian Vegetable Salad, 133
Cooked Dressings, 178–80
    Basic, 178
    Boiled, 178–79
    Boiled, Nova Scotia, 179
    Fruit, 180
    Fruit Whipped Cream, 180
    Oil, 179
    Sherry, 180
Cooked Vegetable Salads, 42–49.
        See also specific vegetables
    Aspic, 83–84
    Basic, 42
    Colombian, 133
    Russian, 137
    Winter, 48
Corn and Chicken Salad, 63
Crab (Crabmeat)
    Bouillabaisse Salad with, 68–69
    Italian Seafood Salad with, 112
    Salad, 70
        in Avocados, 71
        with Thousand Island Dressing, 70
Cracked Wheat and Parsley Salad, 142–43
Cranberry Mold, 88–89
    Orange, 96
Cranberry Orange Salad, 96

Cream Dressing
    Belgian, 189
    for Chicken Salad, 62–63
Creamy Avocado Dressing, 188
Creamy Pink French Dressing, 167
Cucumber and Cucumber Salads
    Appropriate Seasonings, 161
    Aspic, 84
    Chinese, 150
    Dressing, 190
    Eggs Stuffed with, 125–26
    German, 121
    Grated, 53
    Hawaiian Shoyu, 53–54
    Indian, 146
    Moroccan, 142
    Persian, 144
    Scandinavian Eggs Stuffed with, 125–26
    Shredded, 52
    in Sour Cream, 52
    Stuffed, 53
    Turkish, 140
Curly Endive, 25
Curry French Dressing, 164
Curry Powder, 160
Curry Yogurt Dressing, 185

Dairy Dressings, 183–86
    Cottage Cheese, 183
        Buttermilk, 184
        Low-Calorie, 184
    Cream Cheese, 183
    Sour Cream, 184
        Caviar, 185
    Yogurt, 185–86
        Curry, 185
        French, 186
        Low-Calorie, 186
        Mint Low-Calorie, 186
Dandelion, 25
Danish Potato Salad, 125

Dessert Salads, 98–104
    Applesauce Mold, Port, 102
    Apricots with Liqueur, 100
    Broiled Grapefruit, 102–3
    California Fruit, 101
    Double Melon, 99
    Frozen Fruit, 103
        Easy, 104
    Frozen Pineapple, 104
    Fruit as Finger Food, 100
    Fruit Platter, 100–1
    Grapefruit, Broiled, 102–3
    Honeydew Ring Fruit, 98
    Pear Dessert, Hot, 102
    Pineapple, Frozen, 104
    Pineapple Slices Flambé, 103
    Watermelon Bowl, 99
    White Wine Fruit Mold, 101
Deviled Egg Chef's Salad, 39
Dill, 158
Dinner Menus, 20–22
Double Melon Salad, 99
Dressings, 153–93
    Almond Garlic, 187–88
    Avocado, Creamy, 188
    Avocado Mayonnaise, 176
    Bacon, 188
    Blender Mayonnaise, 171
        Green, 174
    Boiled, 178–79
    Bonus, 187–93
    Caper French, 164
    Caper Mayonnaise, 172
    Caraway Mayonnaise, 172
    Catsup French, 164
    Caviar Mayonnaise, 173
    Caviar Sour Cream, 185
    Chicken Liver, 188–89
    Chili Sauce French, 164
    Chive French, 164
    Chive Mayonnaise, 174
    Chutney French, 164
    Cooked, 178–80

Cottage Cheese, 183–84
Cream
    Belgian, 189
    for Chicken Salad, 62–63
Cream Cheese, 183
Creamy Avocado, 188
Creamy Pink French, 167
Cucumber, 190
Curry French, 164
Curry Yogurt, 185
Dairy, 183–86
Egg and Olive French, 166
French, 154, 163–67
Fruit, Cooked, 180
Fruit French, 165
Garlic Almond, 187–88
Garlic French, 165
Green Goddess, 174–75
Green Mayonnaise, 174, 175
Herb French, 164
Herbs, 158–59, 161–62
Herb Wine French, 166
Honey Lemon, 190
Horseradish Herb, 189
India French, 166
Lemon, 190
Lemon French, 165
Lemon Roquefort, 181
Lorenzo, 19
Lorenzo French, 167
Low-Calorie, 184, 186
Mayonnaise, 154, 170–77
Mint, 191
Mint Low-Calorie, 186
Mustard, 191
Mustard French, 166
Mustard Sauce, 49
Parsley French, 164
Red, 192–93
Red Wine, for Shrimp, 74
Remoulade, 193
Roquefort, 181–82
Sardine Mayonnaise, 176

Dressings (cont'd)
  Seafood Sauce, 113
  Sherry, Cooked, 180
  Sherry French, 167
  Sherry Mayonnaise, 175
  Sour Cream, 184
    Caviar, 185
    Cole Slaw with, 54
    for Cucumbers, 52
    Green Goddess Mayonnaise, 175
    for Potato Salad, 118
    Roquefort, 182
  Special, 187
  Spices and Seeds for, 160–62
  Spicy, 192
  Tarragon Mayonnaise, 176
  Tartare Sauce, 177
  Thousand Island, 177
  Water Cress (Lorenzo), 191
    French, 167
  Yogurt, 185–86
    Curry, 185
    French, 186
    Mint, 186

Easy Frozen Fruit Salad, 104
Egg Dressings
  Olive French, 166
  Vinaigrette, 168–69
Eggplant Salads
  Armenian, 140–41
  Mexican, 129
Egg Salads
  Anchovy, Scandinavian, 126
  Appropriate Seasonings for, 161
  Chef's, Deviled, 39
  Cucumber-Stuffed, Scandinavian, 125–26
Endive, Belgian, 25
  Salads, 30–31
Endive, Curly, 25

Escarole, 25

Fennel, 158. See also Finocchio Salad
Field Lettuce, 25
  Salad of, 32
Fines Herbes, 159, 162
Finocchio Salad, 55
Fish Salads, 68–78. See also Chef's Salads; Seafood Salads; specific fish; Shellfish
  Appropriate Seasonings for, 161
  Basic, 69–70
  Bouillabaisse, 68–69
  Ceviche, 130
  Chinese, 149
  Hawaiian Cucumber Shoyu, 53–54
  Niçoise, 77
Flounder Salad, 75
French Dressings, 154, 163–67
  Basic, 163
  Caper, 164
  Catsup, 164
  Chili Sauce, 164
  Chive, 164
  Chutney, 164
  Creamy Pink, 167
  Curry, 164
  Egg and Olive, 166
  Fruit, 165
  Garlic, 165
  Herb, 164
  Herb Wine, 166
  India, 166
  Lemon, 165
  Mustard, 166
  Parsley, 164
  Roquefort, 181
  Sherry, 167
  Variations, 164

French Dressings (cont'd)
  Water Cress, 167
  Yogurt, 186
French Salad Basket, 26
French Salads, 108–10
  Bean and Tomato, 110
  Green, 108
  Mixed Green, 108–9
  Parisian, 109
  Tomato, 110
  Water Cress, 109
Frozen Fruit Salad, 103
  Easy, 104
  Swedish, 124–25
Frozen Pineapple Salad, 104
Fruit Dressings
  Cooked, 180
  French, 165
  Whipped Cream, 180
Fruit Salads, 90–97. See also
    Dessert Salads; specific
    fruits
  Appropriate Seasonings for,
    161
  Beet and, 45
  California, 101
  Finger, 100
  Frozen, 103
    Easy, 104
    Swedish, 124–25
  Honeydew Ring, 98
  Mexican, 131
  Platter, 100–1
  Sunburst, 90
  Swedish Frozen, 124–25
  Waldorf, 95
  White Wine Mold, 101
Frukt Sallad, 124

Garbanzo (Chick Pea) Salad, 47
Garden Lettuce, 25–26
Garlic, 158
  Almond Dressing, 187–88

Crushing, 28
  French Dressing, 165
Gazpacho Salad, 127
German Salads, 118–21
  Cabbage (Cole Slaw), 120
  Cabbage (Red and White),
    119
  Celery, Knob, 120
  Chicken, 121
  Cole Slaw, 120
  Cucumber, 121
  Potato, Hot, 118–19
  Potato, with Sour Cream
    Dressing, 118
  Potato Apple, 119
Grape Almond Salad, 96–97
Grapefruit
  and Avocado Salad, 92 (see
    also Citrus Avocado Salad)
  Mold, 89
  Persimmon and, 92–93
  Broiled, 102–3
Grapes, Bean and Asparagus
    Salad with, 43
Grated Cucumber Salad, 53
Greek Salad, 139
Green Goddess Mayonnaise, 174
  with Sour Cream, 175
Green Mayonnaise, 175
  Blender, 174
Green and Mixed Tossed Salads,
    29–33. For listing, see
    Tossed Salads
  Appropriate Seasonings for,
    161
Greens, 25–27
  with Onions, 30
  Preparing, 26–27
Gurkensalat, 121

Haddock Salad, 69–70
Halibut Salad, 69–70
  Ceviche, 130

Ham, Salad Platter with, 35
Ham Salad, 67. *See also* Chef's
    Salads
    Aspic, 85
    Russian, 137
Hawaiian Cucumber Shoyu
    Salad, 53–54
Hawaiian Stuffed Tomato Salad,
    59
Head Lettuce, 25
Hearts of Palm Salad, 56
    Tomato and, 57
Herbed Tomato Aspic, 82
Herb French Dressing, 164
    Wine, 166
Herb Horseradish Dressing, 189
Herbs, Salad, 158–59
    Appropriate, 161–62
Herring Salad, 122
    Norwegian, 123
Herringsalat, 122
Honeydew Ring Fruit Salad, 98
Honey Lemon Dressing, 190
Horseradish, 160
    Herb Dressing, 189
Hot Pear Dessert, 102
Hot Potato Salad, German, 118–
    19

Iceberg Lettuce, 25
India French Dressing, 166
Indian Cucumber Salad, 146
Insalata di Frutti di Mare, 112
Insalata di Ovoli, 113
Italian Salads, 111–15
    Broccoli Vinaigrette, 115
    Mushroom, 114
    with Mushrooms, 113
    Salad Bowl, 111
    Seafood, 112–13
    Sicilian, 114
    Tomato, 112

Japanese Marinated Mushrooms,
    148
Japanese Turnips and Carrots,
    148

Kartoffelsalat, 118
Knob Celery. *See* Celery Root
    Salad

Lamb's Tongue. *See* Field
    Lettuce
Laurel, 158
Leaf Lettuce, 25–26
Lebanese Potato Salad, 143
Leeks, 158
Leek Salad, 55
    Lettuce and, Swiss, 117
Lemon Dressing, 190
    French, 165
    Honey, 190
    Roquefort, 181
Lemon Mold Roquefort, 88
Lettuce, 25–27. *See also* Tossed
    Salads; specific kinds
    Leek and, Swiss, 117
    Pennsylvania Dutch Wilted,
        33
    Preparing, 26–27
Liang Pan Huang Kua, 150
Light Lemon Roquefort Mold,
    88
Limestone Lettuce, 25
Liqueur, Apricots with, 100
Litchi Avocado Salad, Cambo-
    dian, 147–48
Liver Dressing, Chicken, 188–89
Liver Salad, Chicken, 64
Lobster
    Bouillabaisse Salad with, 68–
        69
    Italian Seafood Salad with,
        112

Lobster (cont'd)
  Salad, 71
    in Avocados, 72
    Basic, 71
    with Mayonnaise, 72
Lorenzo Dressing, 191
  French, 167
Low-Calorie Cottage Cheese
    Dressing, 184
Low-Calorie Yogurt Dressing,
    186
  Mint, 186
Luncheon Menus, 17–19

Macaroni Salad, 80
  Cheddar Bowl, 79
  Platter, 79–80
Marjoram, 158
  Wild, 159
Mayonnaise, 154, 170–77
  Avocado, 176
  Basic, 171
  Blender, 171
    Green, 174
  Caper, 172
  Caraway, 172
  Caviar, 173
  Chive, 174
  Green, 175
    Blender, 174
  Green Goddess, 174
    with Sour Cream, 175
  Sardine, 176
  Sherry, 175
  Tarragon, 176
  Tartare Sauce, 177
  Thousand Island, 177
  Variations, 172
Meat Salads, 66–67. See also
    Chef's Salads; specific meats
  Appropriate Seasonings for,
    161
  Parisian, 109

  Russian, 136–37
Melon Salads
  Double, 99
  Honeydew Ring Fruit, 98
Menus, 17–22
Mexican Eggplant Salad, 129
Mexican Fruit Salad, 131
Mexican Pineapple Coconut
    Salad, 129
Mint, 158
Mint Salad Dressing, 191
  Yogurt Low-Calorie, 186
Mixed and Green Tossed Salads,
    29–33. For listing, see
    Tossed Salads
  Appropriate Seasonings, 161
Molded Salads, 81–89
  Applesauce Port, 102
  Asparagus Mousse, 86
  Avocado Grapefruit, 89
  Beet, Swedish Pickled, 124
  Cheese
    Lemon Roquefort, 88
    Pineapple Mousse, 89
    Roquefort Mousse, 87–88
  Chicken, 63–64
  Cranberry, 88–89
  Cranberry Orange, 96
  Cucumber Aspic, 84
  Grapefruit Avocado, 89
  Ham Aspic, 85
  Lemon Roquefort, 88
  Pineapple Cheese Mousse, 89
  Port Applesauce, 102
  Prune Aspic, 85
  Salmon Mousse, 87
  Tomato Aspic, 83
    Basic, 82
    Herbed, 82
  Tongue in Aspic, 86
  Tuna Mousse, 87
  Vegetable Aspic, 84

Molded Salads (*cont'd*)
  Vegetables in Aspic, 83–84
  White Wine Fruit, 101
Moroccan Cucumber Salad, 142
Mousses, 81, 86–88
  Asparagus, 86
  Pineapple Cheese, 89
  Roquefort, 87–88
  Salmon, 87
  Tuna, 87
Mushrooms
  Celery Salad with, 56
  Italian Salad of, 114
  Italian Salad with, 113
  Japanese Marinated, 148
  Tossed Greens with, 32
Mussels
  Bouillabaisse Salad with, 68–69
  Italian Seafood Salad with, 112
  Potato Salad with, 78
  Remoulade, 77–78
Mustard, 160, 161
  Dressing, 191
    French, 166
    Sauce, 49

Nasturtium, 158
Near Eastern Salads, 139–44
  Cole Slaw, Armenian, 141
  Cracked Wheat and Parsley, 142–43
  Cucumber, Moroccan, 142
  Cucumber, Persian, 144
  Cucumber, Turkish, 140
  Eggplant, Armenian, 140–41
  Greek, 139
  Potato, Lebanese, 143
  Spinach, Persian, 143
  Taramasalata, 139–40
Niçoise Salad, 77
Norwegian Herring Salad, 123

Nova Scotia Boiled Dressing, 179
Nutmeg, 160

Oak Leaf Lettuce, 26
Oils, Salad, 156–57
Olive Anchovy Salad, Spanish, 128
Olive and Egg French Dressing, 166
Olive Oil, 156–57
Olive and Orange Salad, 92
Onion Family, 158
Onion Orange Salad, 91
Onions, Greens with, 30
Orange Salads. *See also* Citrus Avocado Salad
  Celery and, 91
  Cranberry and, 96
    Mold, 96
  Olive and, 92
  Onion and, 91
  Spanish, 127–28
  Water Cress and, 91
Oregano, 159
Oriental Salads, 145–51
  Asparagus, Chinese, 149
  Avocado Litchi, Cambodian, 147–48
  Chicken, Chinese, 151
  Chicken, Singapore, 145
  Cucumber, Chinese, 150
  Cucumber, Indian, 146
  Fish, Chinese, 149
  Mushrooms, Japanese Marinated, 148
  Shrimp, Bangkok, 146–47
  Shrimp, Rangoon, 147
  Tuna, Chinese, 149, 150
  Turnips and Carrots, Japanese, 148
Oysters, Bouillabaisse Salad with, 68–69

Palm Salad, 56
Tomato and, 57
Papas à la Huancaina, 132
Paprika, 160, 161
Parisian Salad, 109
Parsley, 159, 161
and Cracked Wheat Salad, 142–43
French Dressing, 164
Pasta Salads, 78–80
Macaroni, 80
Macaroni Cheddar Bowl, 79
Macaroni Platter, 79–80
Peach Salads
Cheese and, 94
Spicy, 94
Pear Salads
Cheese and, 95
Hot Dessert, 102
Spicy, 94
Waldorf, 95
Pennsylvania Dutch Wilted Lettuce, 33
Pepper, 161
Cayenne, 160
Pepper Salad, Sweet, 138
Persian Cucumber Salad, 144
Persian Spinach Salad, 143
Persimmon, Grapefruit, and Avocado Salad, 92–93
Peruvian Potato Salad, 132
Pickled Beet Mold, Swedish, 124
Pike Salad, Chinese, 149
Pineapple Salads
Cheese Mousse, 89
Coconut and, Mexican, 29
Flambé Slices, 103
Frozen, 104
Platter Salads, 34–35
Macaroni, 79–80
Salad Platter, 35
Vegetable, 34–35
Plum Salad, 97

Poppy Seed Dressing, 192
Poppy Seeds, 161
Port Applesauce Mold, 102
Potato Salad, 60–61
Apple and, Austrian, 119
Appropriate Seasonings for, 162
Danish, 125
Hot German, 118–19
Lebanese, 143
with Mayonnaise, 61
Mussels and, 78
Peruvian, 132
with Sour Cream Dressing, German, 118
Poultry Salads, 62–66. See also specific poultry
Appropriate Seasonings for, 162
Prune Aspic, 85

Radishes, Mixed Green Salad with, 30
Rangoon Shrimp Salad, 147
Raw Vegetable Salads, 50–59. See also Tossed Salads; specific vegetables
Aspic, 84
Platter, 34–35
Red Caviar Mayonnaise, 173
Red Lettuce, 25
Red Pepper Salad. See Pepper Salad
Red Salad Dressing, 192–93
Red and White Cabbage Salad, Austrian, 119
Red Wine, Shrimp with, 74
Remoulade Dressing, 193
Rice Salad, 80
Romaine Lettuce, 26
and Beet Salad, 44
Salad Bowl, 31
Rosemary, 159

Russian Salads, 136–38
  Basic, 136–37
  Ham, 137
  Sweet Pepper, 138
  Vegetable, 137
Russki Salat, 136–37

Salad Bowl Lettuce, 26
Salade de Haricots Verts et
    Tomates, 110
Salmon
  Bouillabaisse Salad with, 68–
    69
  Salad, 76
    Chef's, 38–39
    Mousse, 87
Sardine Mayonnaise, 176
Sausage, Colombian Vegetable
    Salad with, 133
Savory, 159
Scallions, 158, 161
Scallop Salad, Ceviche, 130
Scandinavian Salads, 122–26
  Anchovy Egg, 126
  Beet Mold, Swedish Pickled,
    124
  Egg Anchovy, 126
  Eggs Stuffed with Cucumber,
    125–26
  Fruit, Swedish Frozen, 124–25
  Herring, 122
    Norwegian, 123
  Mixed, Swedish, 123
  Potato, Danish, 125
Seafood Salads. See also Fish Sal-
    ads; specific seafood
  Italian, 112
  Sauce for, 113
Seafood Sauce, 113
Seeds and Spices, 160–61
Shallots, 158
Shellfish. See also Fish Salads;

Seafood    Salads;    specific
    shellfish
  Appropriate Seasonings for,
    161
Sherry Dressing, 180
  French, 167
  Mayonnaise, 175
Shredded Cucumber Salad, 52
Shrimp
  Bouillabaisse Salad with, 68–
    69
  to Cook, 73
  Italian Seafood Salad with,
    112
  Salad, 73–74
    in Avocados, 74
    Bangkok, 146–47
    Chef's, 38
    Rangoon, 147
    with Red Wine, 74
    Vinaigrette, 73
Sicilian Salad, 114
Simpson Lettuce, 25
Singapore Chicken Salad, 145
Sladky Perezs, 138
Sole in Marinade, 75
Sorrel, 159
Sour Cream Dressing, 184
  Caviar, 185
  Cole Slaw with, 54
  Cucumbers in, 52
  Green Goddess Mayonnaise,
    175
  for Potato Salad, 118
  Roquefort, 182
South American Salads, 132–35
  Avocado, 133–34
    Brazilian, 134–35
    Venezuelan Spinach and,
      134
  Potato, Peruvian, 132
  Vegetable, Colombian, 133

Spanish and Mexican Salads, 127–31
  Ceviche, 130
  Eggplant, 129
  Fruit, 131
  Gazpacho, 127
  Olive Anchovy, 128
  Orange, 127–28
  Pineapple Coconut, 129
Special Salad Dressing, 187
Spices and Seeds, 160–61
  Appropriate, 161–62
Spicy Peach or Pear Salad, 94
Spicy Salad Dressing, 192
Spinach, 26
Spinach Salad, 32–33
  Avocado and, Venezuelan, 134
  Bacon and, 33
  Persian, 143
Squid, Italian Seafood Salad with, 112
Stuffed Vegetable Salads. See specific vegetables
Summer Savory, 159
Sunburst Salad, 90
Sunset Salad, 65
Swedish Frozen Fruit Salad, 124–25
Swedish Mixed Salad, 123
Swedish Pickled Beet Mold, 124
Sweetbread Salad, 66
Sweet Marjoram, 158
Sweet Pepper Salad, 138
Swiss Salads, 116–17
  Basic, 116
  Cheese and Anchovy, 116
  Lettuce and Leek, 117

Tabbouleh, 142–43
Taramasalata, 139–40
Tarragon, 159
Tarragon Mayonnaise, 176
Tartare Sauce, 177

Thousand Island Dressing, 177
Three or Four Bean Salad, 42–43
Thyme, 159
Tomato Salad, 57
  Appropriate Seasonings for, 162
  Aspic, 83
    Basic, 82
    Herbed, 82
  Avocado and, 57–58
  Bean and, French, 110
  French, 110
  Hawaiian Stuffed, 59
  Italian, 112
  Palm and, 57
  Stuffed, 58
  Stuffed, Hawaiian, 59
Tongue
  in Aspic, 86
  for Chef's Salad, 36
  Sunset Salad with, 65
Tossed Salads, Green and Mixed, 29–33
  Appropriate Seasonings for, 161
  Endive, 30–31
  Field Salad, 32
  Green, 29
    Mixed, 29–30
    Mixed French, 108–9
    Mixed Swedish, 123
  Greens and Mushrooms, 32
  Greens with Onions, 29
  Mixed Green, 29
    French, 108–9
    with Radishes, 30
    Swedish, 123
  Mushroom Greens, 32
  Romaine Salad Bowl, 31
  Spinach, 32–33
    Bacon and, 33
  Wilted Lettuce, Pennsylvania Dutch, 33

Tossing of Salad, 156
Tuna Salad, 76
  Cheese and, 76–77
  Chinese, 149, 150
  Mousse, 87
  Niçoise, 77
Turbot Salad, 69–70
Turkey Salad, 64–65
Turkish Cucumber Salad, 140
Turnips and Carrots, Japanese, 148

Veal Salads
  Parisian, 109
  Russian, 136–37
Vegetable Salads
  Appropriate Seasonings for, 162
  Cooked, 42–49. See also specific vegetables
    Aspic, 83–84
    Basic, 42
    Colombian, 133
    Russian, 137
    Winter, 48
  Raw, 50–59. See also Tossed Salads; specific vegetables
    Aspic, 84
    Platter, 34–35
Venezuelan Avocado and Spinach Salad, 134
Vinaigrette, 168–69
  Egg, 168–69
Vinegar, 157

Waldorf Salad, 95
  Pear, 95

Washing of Greens, 26–27
Water Cress, 26
  Dressing (Lorenzo), 191
    French, 167
  Salad, 109
    Orange and, 91
Watermelon
  Double Melon Salad, 99
  Salad Bowl, 99
Wheat Pilaf and Parsley Salad, 142–43
Whipped Cream Fruit Dressing, 180
White Wine Fruit Mold, 101
Wild Marjoram, 159
Wilted Lettuce, Pennsylvania Dutch, 33
Wine. See also Sherry Dressing
  Applesauce Mold, Port, 102
  French Dressing, Herb, 166
  French Dressing, Sherry, 167
  Fruit Mold, White, 101
  Shrimp with Red, 74
Wine Vinegar, 157
Winter Salad, 48
Winter Savory, 159
Woodruff, 159

Yogurt Dressings, 185–86
  Curry, 185
  French, 186
  Low-Calorie, 186
  Mint Low-Calorie, 186

Zucchini Salad, 60
  with Vegetables, 59